Earthquake cycle research with satellites

Nathan R. Hicks

To my family

ABSTRACT

The motion of the Earth's tectonic plates creates a gradual accumulation of stress at their boundaries, followed by a rapid release in earthquakes, a process known as the earthquake cycle. Studying this process is important because of the hazards earthquakes pose, but presents challenges due to the multi-scale nature of the problem—stresses build up over hundreds to thousands of years, while earthquakes break narrow fault zones in a matter of seconds. In this thesis, we combine a variety of techniques to study the earthquake cycle on multiple temporal and spatial scales, including satellite-based interferometric synthetic aperture radar (InSAR) to observe the slow deformation of the Earth over wide areas, and high-performance computational simulations to model faults during earthquakes. We begin by presenting a method for removing the signal of plate-tectonic motion in large-scale InSAR measurements, allowing for better observation of small ground deformations. We then use these corrections to study the Makran subduction zone, on the Iran-Pakistan border. Our InSAR-derived ground velocity map can resolve motions at the level of millimeters per year over an area of nearly one million square kilometers, and we use it to place constraints on the degree of coupling on the subduction megathrust. Next, we show how InSAR can be combined with deep learning techniques to rapidly map earthquake damage in all weather conditions, day and night. Such products will hopefully prove useful in future disaster response. Finally, we present computational simulations of dynamic earthquake ruptures with enhanced dynamic weakening due to thermal pressurization. We apply our simplified model to the creeping section of the San Andreas Fault, which is generally thought to be a barrier to earthquake rupture. Our results show how thermal pressurization can allow earthquakes to propagate partially or completely through the creeping section for a range of physically reasonable parameters. Our work illustrates how results from multiple fields can be combined to deliver new insights into the earthquake cycle and the hazards that it poses.

TABLE OF CONTENTS

LIST OF ILLUSTRATIONS

LIST OF TABLES

INTRODUCTION

0.1 Background

Why do earthquakes happen? The Greek philosopher Aristotle (384-322 BCE) thought the culprit was the escape of evaporating water from the Earth, while for the ancient Chinese, who made the first written records of earthquakes, such events were the sign of an imbalance between heaven and Earth, and a harbinger of the ruling dynasty's fall from power (Needham, 1959). In 132 CE, the Chinese polymath Zhang Heng (78-139 CE) created the first seismoscope, a device that allowed the direction of distant earthquakes to be measured, even when seismic waves were imperceptible. The seismoscope could help the government dispatch relief to the affected areas; however, the underlying cause of earthquakes remained elusive.

In 1755, the Portuguese city of Lisbon was hit by a devastating earthquake and tsunami, triggering political and philosophical upheavals across Europe. The event was notable in the history of seismology for the detailed surveying of the shaking and damage, directed by the Portuguese chief minister, the Marquis of Pombal (1699-1782).[1] While interpreted as a sign of God's wrath, the disaster also prompted more naturalistic explanations, such as German philosopher Emmanuel Kant's (1724-1804) proposal that earthquakes were produced by the reaction of sulphur and ion with water in caverns beneath the Earth's surface (Reinhardt & Oldroyd, 1983).

It was not until 1910 that a key element in our modern understanding of earthquakes fell into place. In 1906, a rupture along the San Andreas Fault, in California, badly damaged the city of San Francisco. Harry Fielding Reid (1859-1944), professor of geology at Johns Hopkins University, found that the ground surface along the San Andreas Fault had deformed in the 50 years before the earthquake. Reid proposed that this deformation, or "strain," stored energy in the rocks beneath the surface, which was then released in the devastating earthquake: the "elastic-rebound theory" (Reid, 1910).

Reid's theory allowed him to suggest how future earthquakes could be predicted, by measuring where and by how much the Earth was deforming:

> "As strains always precede the rupture and as the strains are sufficiently
> great to be easily detected before the rupture occurs, in order to foresee

---

[1]Technically he did not gain the "Marquis of Pombal" title until 1769.

tectonic earthquakes it is merely necessary to devise a method of deter-
mining the existence of the strains; and the rupture will in general occur
in the neighborhood of the line where the strains are greatest, or along
an older fault-line where the rock is weakest" (Reid (1910), p. 31).

Reid went on to suggest a method for how this deformation could be measured:

"To measure the growth of strains, we should build a line of piers, say
a kilometer apart, at right angles to the direction which a geological
examination of the region, or past experience, indicates the fault will
take when the rupture occurs; a careful determination from time to time,
of the directions of the lines joining successive piers, their differences
of level, and the exact distance between them, would reveal any strains
which might be developing along the region the line of piers crosses"
(Reid (1910), p. 31).

Reid was only able to speculate as to what was driving the deformation of the Earth,
suggesting that "flows below the surface may have been the origin of the forces we
have been considering" (Reid (1910), p. 27). In 1912, German meteorologist Alfred
Wegener proposed "continental drift," the idea that the present continents had once
been part of a single land mass, and had slowly drifted apart. By the 1960s, this
idea had developed into the modern theory of plate tectonics: the brittle outer layer
of the Earth (the lithosphere[2]) is divided up into plates that slowly move past each
other at a few centimeters per year (McKenzie & Parker, 1967). At their boundaries,
the plates are stuck together, and so slowly bend as they move, storing up energy
which is then released in earthquakes. The combination of the steady forcing from
plate motion, with regular elastic rebound during earthquakes, suggests the idea
of an "earthquake cycle", a potentially periodic repetition of stress build up (the
"inter-seismic" phase) followed by stress release (the "co-seismic" phase).

The picture of the Earth storing up elastic energy in the lithosphere, which is
then released in earthquakes along faults (planes of weakness in the Earth), is
complicated by more detailed observations of fault behavior. Faults do not just
slip during earthquakes, they can also move slowly, at a speed of millimeters per

---

[2]In this introduction, I will use the terms "crust" and "lithosphere" interchangeably. This is
technically incorrect—the lithosphere is the rigid outer layer of our planet, while the crust is the
upper part of the lithosphere that is distinguished by its chemical composition. Sue me ☺

year, in a process known as "creep." These observations can be explained by dividing faults into "velocity-strengthening" and "velocity-weakening" regions (e.g., Scholz (1998)). Velocity-strengthening sections of faults become stronger as the stresses build up and cause the fault to slip more quickly. Such strengthening behavior should make the fault unable to host earthquakes; fast slip on the fault causes a dramatic increase in strength, which rapidly slows any rupture. Within this model, velocity-strengthening sections should deform only by creep and act as barriers to earthquakes. Velocity-weakening sections, on the other hand, are "seismogenic"—they can rupture in earthquakes. With a build up in stress, the fault begins to move, growing weaker as it does. Such weakening allows it to slip faster, creating more weakening in a feedback loop that results in an earthquake. After this sudden slip, the fault becomes locked, once again storing up energy to be released in a future earthquake.

Measurements of the Earth's surface allow us to identify regions of faults that are slowly creeping, and those that are locked (e.g., Burgmann (2000)). For example, we can divide the San Andreas Fault into locked sections in the north (where the 1906 earthquake occurred) and south, separated by a 140-km-long creeping section (e.g., Jolivet et al. (2015)). These measurements are easiest where faults are well exposed on land, as they are for the San Andreas, and are more challenging for offshore faults, such as the gigantic "megathrust" faults found at subduction zones, where one of the Earth's plates slides under the other. Nevertheless, if we are able to identify the locked and creeping areas of faults, as well as the rate at which energy is being stored in the crust around the fault, such measurements can offer some indication of where, and how big, an earthquake might be (e.g., Avouac (2015)).

There are, however, numerous factors that further complicate this model. For example, not all energy that is used to deform the rock is necessarily recovered during the earthquake—some amount can be used in creating permanent crustal deformation, both during the inter-seismic and co-seismic phases, as well as during a "post-seismic" phase of deformation triggered by the earthquake (e.g., Avouac (2015), Johnson (2013), Perfettini and Avouac (2004), Shen et al. (1994), and K. Wang et al. (2021)). The straightforward division of faults into velocity-strengthening and velocity-weakening areas, leading to creeping and seismogenic behavior, respectively, is also being increasingly challenged by observations and experiments showing that apparently velocity-strengthening materials can dramatically weaken when driven at fast slip rates, a process known as "dynamic weakening" (Di Toro et al., 2011; Tsutsumi & Shimamoto, 1997; Tullis, 2007). If velocity-strengthening patches can undergo dynamic weakening, then the idea that they represent barriers to earthquake rupture is in doubt (Noda & Lapusta, 2013).

Because of such complexities, understanding the earthquake cycle requires studying the Earth over many scales of time and space. The stresses in the Earth are built up by planetary scale motions of the Earth's lithosphere, which can load faults for hundreds to thousands of years between major earthquakes. While the interseismic loading can span many human lifetimes, the co-seismic rupture is orders of magnitude faster—the rupture propagates at kilometers per second, with meters of slip accumulating in just a few seconds (Heaton, 1990). During this rupture, dynamic weakening can allow faults to go from apparent barriers to earthquake rupture to dramatically weaker in a fraction of a second, and the width of the fault zone that slips can be tiny, as small as micrometers by some estimates (e.g., Chester and Chester (1998) and Platt et al. (2014)).

To do such multi-scale work, geoscientists must combine many fields of study. Geodesy, or the measurement of the shape of Earth's surface, can tell us about the deformation of the Earth over decades. In 1910, Reid was limited to the results of ground-based triangulation surveys of fixed locations before and after the earthquake. The development of space-based geodetic techniques, such as Global Navigation Satellite Systems (GNSS) and Interferometric Synthetic Aperture Radar (InSAR) now allow us to measure motions of millimeters per year, with dense temporal sampling, on a global scale (Blewitt, 2015; Simons & Rosen, 2015). These techniques can provide high resolution imaging of each stage of the earthquake cycle, from inter-seismic strain accumulation, to co-seismic offsets and post-seismic deformation (e.g., Avouac (2015), Fialko et al. (2001), Hsu et al. (2006), and Simons et al. (2011)).

Geodesy alone can only give us information over the time scales of the surveys. Given that the interval between large earthquakes on particular faults can be centuries, it is necessary to look to other techniques to gain a fuller understanding of the history of each fault—i.e., when and how big its previous earthquakes were. Large earthquakes can cause several meters of slip and alter the rocks and soil surrounding the fault. The field of paleoseismology searches for signs of these processes to create histories of previous earthquakes on major faults, potentially going back thousands of years (e.g., Sieh (1978b) and Sieh et al. (1989)). Geological investigations of fault zones can be used to understand the total amount of slip on the fault, and how that slip was accommodated, over millions of years (e.g., Chester and Chester (1998))

The work described above is primarily observational—it relies on recording and understanding natural phenomena, rather than controlling them. Experiments present an alternative approach; taking samples, potentially obtained directly from fault zones, and measuring how they respond under different conditions. For example, scientists can adjust the pressure and water saturation conditions of a fault sample, and see how this affects its frictional strength at different sliding velocities, searching for signs of dynamic weakening (French et al., 2014). The controlled conditions of the laboratory allows for measurements on the scale of micrometers and microseconds (e.g., Rubino et al. (2022)), providing insights that are impossible to obtain directly from faults buried deep beneath the Earth's surface.

The combination of observation and experimentation presents a messy, tangled picture of the physical processes acting in the Earth. It is the job of modeling to take this picture and reduce it to understandable parameters that give some insight into the physical processes that are acting. A classic example is Newton's second law, which takes a series of observations of the world, from pushing a glass across a table, to the orbit of the Earth around the Sun, and unifies them under one theoretical model: $F = ma$. This equation tells us that the acceleration of a body (a) is equal to the net force we apply (F), divided by its mass (m), and allows us to explain how bodies move in response to forces. In a similar fashion, Reid's elastic rebound theory reduced observations of ground deformation along the San Andreas fault into a model of energy stored in and then released from an elastic crust.

Just as an experimentalist measures how their samples respond to different conditions in the laboratory, models can be experimented with by varying their parameters and calculating the output, then comparing the results with real-world observations. When models are sufficiently complex, this experimentation can only be done with the aid of computer simulations. For example, when studying the earthquake cycle, computer simulations can be used to understand how the addition of dynamic weakening to velocity-weakening and velocity-strengthening patches could affect fault behavior over thousands of years, and compare these outputs with observed earthquakes (Cubas et al., 2015; Noda & Lapusta, 2013).

0.2 Thesis Overview

In this thesis, we draw on insights from a wide range of observational, experimental, computational and theoretical studies to better understand different components of the earthquake cycle. We focus our attention on geodetic measurements from InSAR, computational simulations of earthquake rupture, and theoretical understanding of these simulations.

We begin by discussing long-wavelength signals in InSAR measurements of ground velocity (Chapter 1). InSAR is a powerful technique for measuring ground deformation over wide areas; however, the data often contains contaminating signals that limit the ability of InSAR alone to measure deformation over hundreds of kilometers. This issue is generally solved by combining InSAR with GNSS measurements to constrain long-wavelength deformation. We demonstrate that the movement of the Earth's tectonic plates creates long-wavelength signals in InSAR measurements that could potentially be misinterpreted as deformation, and show how to remove them using plate motion models.

Using the plate-motion corrections, we apply InSAR data to measure ground deformation over the Makran subduction zone, a 1000 km long megathrust where the Arabian plate slides beneath the Eurasian plate on the Iran-Pakistan border (Chapter 2). The approach is similar in spirit to Reid's 1910 proposal to understand the earthquake cycle by measuring strain accumulation, but we have the advantage of 110 years of progress in geodesy. We are able to resolve on-going post-seismic deformation, co-seismic offsets, and rapid ground subsidence due to aquifer discharge over an area of nearly one million square kilometers using 7.5 years of InSAR data, without the aid of GNSS. Of particular interest is the degree of "coupling" on the subduction zone—i.e., how much of the motion between the plates is stored as elastic energy that could be released in future earthquakes. Our measurements do not allow us to unambiguously resolve the degree of coupling, but we use simple elastic models to place constraints on the strength of coupling and compare the results to previous studies.

In Chapter 3 we follow in the footsteps of Zhang Heng and the Marquis of Pombal by developing a method to rapidly map earthquake damage over wide areas using InSAR satellites. Using large amounts of InSAR data, combined with modern deep-learning techniques, our method can locate collapsed buildings within hours to days after major disasters, which could help to direct emergency response, particularly in remote areas. The use of InSAR means that our method works day and night, and in all weather conditions.

For the final chapter, we shift our attention to high-performance computational simulations of earthquake rupture (Chapter 4). Building on work by Noda and Lapusta (2013) and Cubas et al., 2015, we explore the conditions under which dynamic weakening can allow creeping faults to rupture in earthquakes. We focus on a dynamic weakening process known as "thermal pressurization" (Sibson, 1973), and use our model to simulate the behavior of the creeping section of the San Andreas Fault as we vary the efficiency of weakening. We find that thermal pressurization could allow for ruptures to propagate through the creeping section within our simplified model, potentially allowing ruptures to grow much larger than would be expected if the creeping section was a barrier to earthquake rupture.

We finish with some conclusions and suggestions for future directions of research.

Chapter 1

THE IMPACT OF PLATE MOTIONS ON LONG-WAVELENGTH INSAR-DERIVED VELOCITY FIELDS

1.1 Introduction

Interferometric Synthetic Aperture Radar (InSAR) is an active imaging technique for measuring ground displacements that occur between repeat passes of an imaging platform, such as a satellite (e.g., Hanssen (2001), Massonnet and Feigl (1998), and Simons and Rosen (2015)). InSAR deformation measurements are generally expressed relative to a single point, or ensemble of points, within the imaged area, usually assumed to be stable through time (e.g., Mahapatra et al. (2018)). While InSAR has been used extensively for measuring large amplitude (> 1 cm), deformation over short-wavelengths (< 100 km) (e.g., Massonnet et al. (1993) and Merryman Boncori (2019)), other signals present in the data challenge our ability to measure deformation at the scale of millimeters per year over hundreds of kilometers.

InSAR observations at long wavelengths are the combination of motion of the Earth's surface, changes in the atmosphere, and measurement and processing errors. The Earth motion signals comprise the surface deformation of interest, e.g., from tectonic strain, volcanic activity or subsidence (Amelung et al. (1999), Massonnet and Feigl (1998), and Massonnet et al. (1993)), along with solid Earth tides (SET) (X. Xu & Sandwell, 2020), and ocean tidal loading (Dicaprio et al., 2008). Atmospheric signals come from propagation delay through the ionosphere (Z.-W. Xu et al., 2004) and troposphere (Tarayre & Massonnet, 1996). Error sources include the satellite orbits (Massonnet & Feigl, 1998), local oscillator drift (Marinkovic & Larsen, 2015), phase unwrapping (Biggs et al., 2007) and topography (Berardino et al., 2002).

These effects can obscure small amplitude, long-wavelength signals in InSAR due to local tectonic processes, such as surface deformation from interseismic loading (e.g., Fournier et al. (2011) and Parizzi et al. (2021)). Thus, it is common to not interpret long-wavelength signals from InSAR alone, instead removing them by empirically fitting 2D polynomial functions, known as "ramps", to the data (e.g., Fialko (2006) and Jolivet et al. (2015)), or combining InSAR velocities with Global Navigation Satellite System (GNSS) measurements in order to constrain the long-wavelength deformation (e.g., Neely et al. (2020), Parizzi et al. (2020), Weiss et al.

(2020), and X. Xu et al. (2021)). Such approaches are limiting when we wish to measure large-scale deformation in regions of sparse GNSS coverage (Chaussard et al., 2016; Neely et al., 2020).

The quality of InSAR data and correction methods have substantially increased over the last several years. The European Space Agency's (ESA) Sentinel-1 satellites have been regularly acquiring data for significant portions of the planet since late 2014. Sentinel-1 offers the advantages of improved orbital controls and uncertainties, reducing the noise contribution from satellite orbits (Fattahi & Amelung, 2014), as well as unrestricted data access. Split-band processing now allows for the estimation of the ionospheric signal directly from the InSAR data (Fattahi, Simons, et al., 2017; Gomba et al., 2016; Liang et al., 2019), and higher quality weather models have improved the correction of the tropospheric phase (Doin et al., 2009; Jolivet et al., 2011; Z. Li et al., 2005). Techniques for removing the SET (X. Xu & Sandwell, 2020) and ocean tidal loading signals (Dicaprio et al., 2008; Yu et al., 2020) have also been developed, among other correction methods. After corrections, there may still be long-wavelength residuals in multi-year Sentinel-1 time series, including from the troposphere, which can contribute up to 5 mm/yr over 150 km (Parizzi et al., 2021), and orbital errors, contributing around 0.5 mm/yr over 100 km for Sentinel-1 (Fattahi & Amelung, 2014).

In this work, we focus on the contribution of coherent uniform motion of Earth's tectonic plates to the long-wavelength component of InSAR-derived velocity fields. The satellite line-of-sight (LOS) vector varies systematically in the satellite range direction (i.e., across the satellite track), causing a changing sensitivity to ground deformation with range. Bulk motion of tectonic plates in the satellite frame of reference, coupled with this LOS variation, can create quasi-linear gradients in InSAR-derived velocity fields, resulting in ramps, predominantly in the satellite range direction. This effect has been noted before, e.g., by Bähr et al. (2012), Bähr (2013) and Parizzi et al. (2020). Here, we demonstrate that plate motion creates ramps of several millimeters per year, across the 250 km track width, in six multi-year Sentinel-1 InSAR time series. After other corrections have been applied, plate motion is the dominant long-wavelength signal in our data, and we show that this signal can be straightforwardly compensated for using plate motion models. This adjustment is not currently part of several open-source InSAR time series analysis packages (e.g., Agram et al. (2013), Hooper et al. (2012), Morishita et al. (2020), and Yunjun et al. (2019)), and we provide an implementation of the method in the MintPy package (Yunjun et al., 2019).

1.2 The Reference Frame of InSAR Measurements

Quantifying ground deformation using InSAR requires a precise measurement of the satellite orbit ephemerides (Fattahi & Amelung, 2014; Peter, 2021). For Sentinel-1 the orbit is measured with respect to the International Terrestrial Reference Frame (ITRF) (Peter, 2021), an Earth-centered, Earth-fixed reference frame in which there is no net rotation of the Earth's surface (Altamimi et al., 2016). Observations of absolute ground motion relative to the satellite are therefore also in ITRF (Bähr et al., 2012; Lazecky & Hooper, 2022).

However, it is not possible for InSAR to record absolute motions due to the 2π ambiguity in the interferometric phase (e.g., Massonnet and Feigl (1998)). Instead, displacement measurements are generally expressed relative to a reference point within the imaged region, assumed to be stationary. Velocities can then be obtained from functional fits to displacement time series, with inferred velocities also expressed relative to this point.

Selecting the reference point is not equivalent to expressing the InSAR velocities in a reference frame moving with that point (Bähr, 2013; Bähr et al., 2012). We must therefore consider how velocities in ITRF appear in the InSAR deformation field. We represent the 3D ITRF secular velocity field of the Earth's surface as:

$$v(x) = v_p(x) + v_d(x). \tag{1.1}$$

$v_p(x)$ is the velocity field due to the strain-free motion of the relevant rigid plate in ITRF, and $v_d(x)$ is the velocity due to internal deformation of the plate, for example due to tectonic, volcanic, or hydrological processes.

Defining the LOS unit vector pointing from the ground to the satellite as $\hat{l}(x)$, the LOS projection of the 3D velocity field, minus the InSAR reference velocity, can be written as:

$$v_l(x) = v(x) \cdot \hat{l}(x) - v(x') \cdot \hat{l}(x'), \tag{1.2}$$

where the reference is at point x'. $v_l(x)$ is the secular velocity that will be measured by the satellite, assuming all other signals and noise can be neglected.

In ITRF, $v_l(x)$ has a contribution from the plate motion, which we can write as:

$$v_{l,p}(x) = v_p(x) \cdot \hat{l}(x) - v_p(x') \cdot \hat{l}(x'). \tag{1.3}$$

The second term, from the reference, is constant, while the first term depends on the spatial variation of $v_p(x)$ and $\hat{l}(x)$. The LOS vector $\hat{l}(x)$ can vary substantially over an image swath. For Sentinel-1, the incidence angle (the angle between the LOS and the vertical) varies approximately from $29°$ in the near range to $46°$ in the far range over the 250 km width of the imaging swath (for data acquired in Interferometric Wideswath mode). The range-dependent variation in $\hat{l}(x)$ implies a changing sensitivity to components of the 3D deformation field across the track, with sensitivity to horizontal motion increasing and vertical motion decreasing as we move from near range to far range. This range-dependent sensitivity causes uniform plate motions to appear as velocity ramps in the range direction when projected into the satellite LOS (Figure 1.1).

The plate velocity, $v_p(x)$, also varies over an image swath. The motion of a rigid plate on Earth's surface can be represented by a rotation rate about an axis, known as an Euler pole (McKenzie & Parker, 1967). Given the angular velocity of a chosen plate, Ω, we can write the velocity of any point, x, on that plate as $v_p(x) = \Omega \times x$, where $\times$ is the cross product. Thus, the velocity field due to rigid plate motion varies with distance from the plate's Euler pole. This variation in $v_p(x)$ also contributes to the long-wavelength LOS velocity field.

Because of the effect of plate motions, InSAR velocity measurements should not generally be considered to be in a local reference frame, despite the use of a local reference point. Choosing a reference point within an InSAR image offsets InSAR velocity measurements from the LOS projection of ITRF velocities by an unknown constant (Equation 1.1), but does not remove the long-wavelength gradients that can be induced by plate motion (Equation 1.3). If ITRF plate motion is negligible when projected to the LOS, and does not vary substantially over the InSAR track, or the satellite LOS variation across the track is small, then $v_{l,p}(x) \approx 0$. Choosing a reference point that is stable with respect to the plate is then approximately equivalent to putting the InSAR velocities into the reference frame of that plate; however, this should not be generally assumed.

Several authors have investigated the reference frame of InSAR observations, generally in the context of using GNSS to put InSAR measurements into a terrestrial reference frame (e.g., Johnston et al. (2021) and Mahapatra et al. (2018)). The influence of plate motion on InSAR velocities has been noted by Bähr et al. (2012) and Bähr (2013), who term it the *reference frame effect*. Bähr et al. (2012) present this phenomenon in terms of a temporally increasing correction to the interferometric

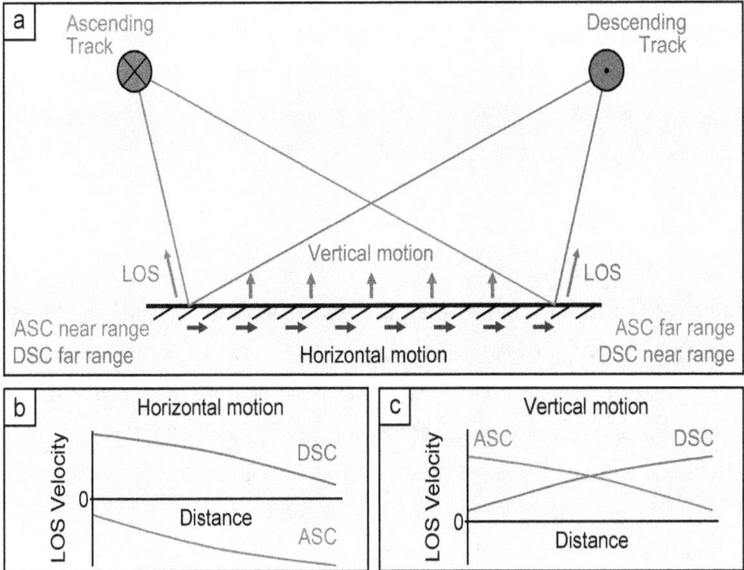

Figure 1.1:   Illustration of how uniform horizontal and vertical motions result in ramps in InSAR-derived velocity measurements. (**a**) Satellite images acquired from ascending (ASC) and descending (DSC) orbital tracks, which have a varying LOS incidence angle across the track. The term "range" refers to the distance from the ground target to the satellite, with near range and far range the closest and furthest points from the satellite, respectively. Red and blue arrows represent the ground-to-satellite LOS vector in the near range for ASC and DSC tracks, respectively. Grey and black arrows represent plate motion in the reference frame of the satellite. For illustration purposes we assume the ASC and DSC tracks are parallel to each other but in opposite directions, and ignore Earth curvature. Figure not to scale. (**b**) Profile of the horizontal plate velocity projected into the LOS of the ASC and DSC tracks, against geographic distance along the ground. (**c**) Same as (b), except for vertical plate motion, resulting in opposite gradients in the LOS profiles. The observing geometry creates a small curvature in all profiles, which is exaggerated in the figure. For InSAR measurements, the LOS velocity is expressed relative to a point within the image, so each of these profiles would be vertically shifted to intersect with the x axis at the chosen reference point.

baseline, while Bähr (2013) notes that this can also be framed in terms of the varying satellite LOS causing differing sensitivity to plate motion (the approach taken here). Parizzi et al. (2020) used plate motion models to adjust their LOS velocity fields after merging InSAR with GNSS. Authors have also noted the impact of plate motions on SAR geolocation accuracy (Cong et al. (2012)). Our focus here is to demonstrate that plate motions can explain a significant fraction of observed residual long-wavelength surface velocities, after other corrections have been applied, and without combining InSAR data with GNSS.

1.3 Data and Methods

1.3.1 Data Processing

We present several examples using InSAR data from the ESA's Sentinel-1 satellites, taken from ascending (ASC) and descending (DSC) tracks covering the Makran subduction zone (Iran), the Gulf of Aqaba (at the northern end of the Red Sea), and western Australia. For each track, we process at least 5 years of data using the InSAR Scientific Computing Environment (ISCE) (Fattahi, Agram, et al., 2017; Rosen et al., 2012). After forming the interferogram networks, we create deformation time series using MintPy (Yunjun et al., 2019).

Before examining residual signals due to plate motion, we apply corrections for the ionosphere, troposphere, SET, and digital elevation model (DEM) error. We use split-band processing to correct for the ionosphere (Liang et al., 2019), PyAPS and the ERA5 weather model to mitigate the tropospheric delay (Hersbach et al., 2020; Jolivet, Agram, et al., 2014), the method of Fattahi and Amelung (2013) for DEM error correction and PySolid to correct for SET (Milbert, 2018; Yunjun et al., 2022). Further details of our data and processing are presented in Appendix A (Sections A.2, A.3, and Table A.1).

1.3.2 Adjusting InSAR Measurements for Plate Motion

After all other corrections have been applied, we can then observe and account for the signal of plate motion. InSAR observations of ground motion are generally used to study regional deformation, rather than plate translations or rotations. For such purposes, a useful reference frame is one that moves with the plate in which we are trying to measure strain. Translating into this reference frame requires us to remove the signal of plate motion in the satellite's frame of reference, i.e., ITRF (Bähr, 2013; Parizzi et al., 2020).

GNSS networks can be used to connect InSAR measurements to ITRF (e.g., Johnston et al. (2021) and Mahapatra et al. (2018)), which can then be transformed into a reference frame moving with the chosen plate. In the absence of sufficient GNSS coverage, we can estimate the transformation into the plate's frame of reference using the following steps:

1. Choose an InSAR reference point, x', that is stable with respect to the plate

2. Find the velocity field of the plate within ITRF, i.e., $v_p(x)$

3. Project that velocity field into the satellite LOS direction

4. Subtract the LOS velocity of the reference point, $v_{l,p}(x')$, from the projected plate velocity to compute $v_{l,p}(x)$, which is then removed from the InSAR velocity map.

Note that, after these steps, InSAR-derived velocities are still expressed relative to a reference point, meaning that deformation and other signals seen at the reference point will still affect the entire scene.

We use the geodetically constrained ITRF plate motion model of Altamimi et al. (2017) to estimate the plate velocity field. For each study region, we identify our reference plate (Table A.1), then use the modeled angular velocity of the plate to calculate horizontal velocities for our observation region. We then project these velocities into the LOS direction and remove them from the velocity map.

1.4   Results

1.4.1   The Importance of Removing Other Signals for Revealing Plate Motion

We expect plate motion to contribute below 8 mm/yr across the 250 km width of the Sentinel-1 tracks for our chosen regions (Figure A.6), making it important to remove other signals to show what fraction of the residual velocity can be explained by plate motion. For ASC tracks in the Makran and Gulf of Aqaba, ionosphere corrections have a particularly large effect on the long-wavelength velocity signal (e.g., contributing a 25 mm/yr ramp along track 86 for the Makran, Figure 1.2), with DSC tracks showing substantially less ionospheric signal. ASC tracks are acquired at dusk—a period of greater ionosphere activity than dawn, when DSC tracks are acquired. This impact is still notable in C-band Sentinel-1 data, even though it suffers much less from ionospheric effects than L-band (Fattahi, Simons, et al., 2017; Liang et al., 2019).

We find that troposphere corrections have a less significant impact on the long-wavelength velocity signal than the ionosphere for ASC tracks, and a comparable effect for DSC tracks. Corrections for the SET have a small effect on the long-wavelength secular velocity, contributing below 0.5 mm/yr over several hundred kilometers. The range of DEM error corrections is less than ±0.5 mm/yr in our results and has a minimal contribution to the long-wavelength velocity field. We show the impact of the above corrections for all tracks in Figures 1.2 and A.1-A.5, and present more details in Section A.3.

1.4.2 The Impact of Accounting for Plate Motion

After applying the suite of corrections we are left with residual velocity ramps in all of our tracks, predominantly in the range direction. We present the results of plate motion adjustments for several tracks in Figures 1.3 and 1.4. Our results show that accounting for plate motion removes a significant fraction of the residual velocity ramp in every case, reducing the across-track ramps from 4-7 mm/yr/track to below 1.5 mm/yr/track. For our data the plate motion signal is comparable to the troposphere in its effect on the long-wavelength velocity field.

The proximity of the Arabian plate Euler pole to the Gulf of Aqaba study area results in the plate velocity field varying appreciably within the tracks (Altamimi et al., 2017). This variation causes an additional LOS velocity ramp along the track, with an opposite direction for the ascending and descending tracks. Figures 1.4 (a) and (b) show how this along-track gradient can be clearly seen in the data, and is well corrected for by the plate motion model. We do not see similar along-track ramps for Australia and Makran, which is consistent with the plate motion velocity field.

1.5 Discussion

Other authors have previously noted that plate motion will affect InSAR velocity measurements (e.g., Bähr et al. (2012)). However, the narrower variation of the satellite LOS angle for earlier satellites, more limited data, and the presence of other significant long-wavelength signals, has made the signal difficult to isolate. The quality of recently available data and correction methods, and the wide swath of Sentinel-1, allow us to show the plate motion signal and the clear impact of accounting for it. Our results from the Gulf of Aqaba illustrate that plate rotation is an important part of the correction.

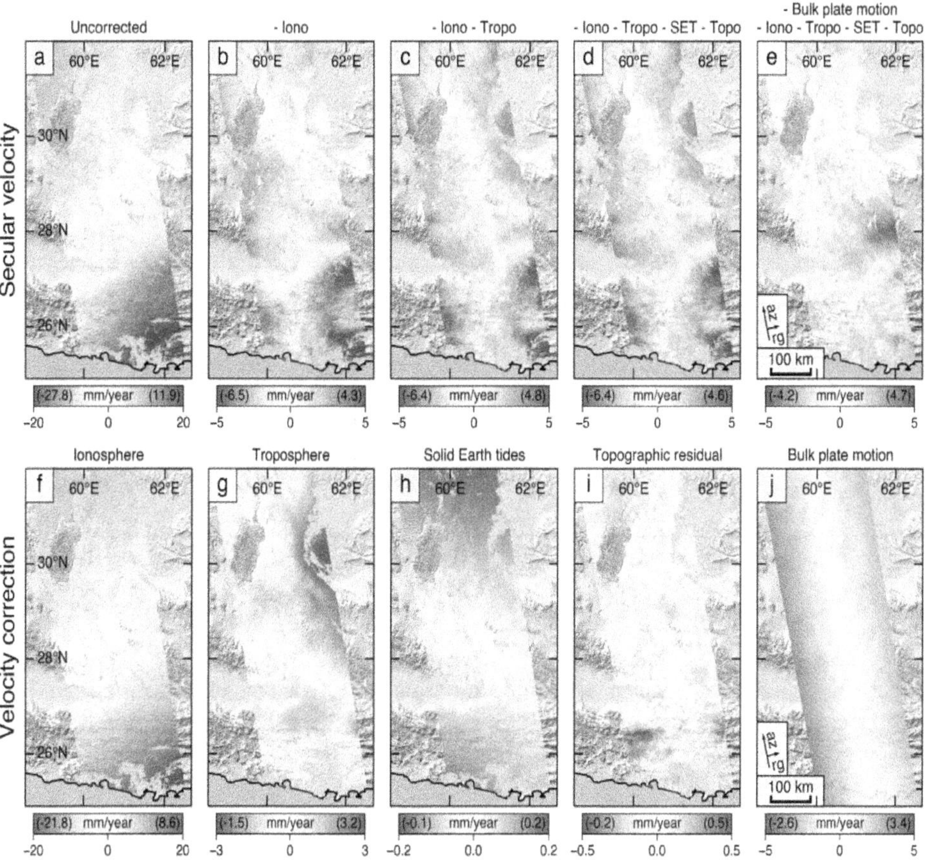

Figure 1.2: Cumulative impact of corrections on the InSAR-derived velocity field for Sentinel-1, track 86 (ASC) over the Makran subduction zone. For plotting purposes, we remove the median value from each velocity field. Positive values represent apparent motion towards the satellite. Color bars are re-scaled between plots. Numbers in parentheses within the color bars refer to the 2nd and 98th percentiles of the velocity. "az" is the azimuth direction (satellite direction of motion), and "rg" the range direction (perpendicular to the satellite direction of motion). **(a)** No corrections applied. **(b)** Estimated ionosphere removed. **(c)** Tropospheric model removed. **(d)** SET model removed and DEM error (Topo) correction applied. **(e)** Plate motion correction applied. The positive signal around (28 °N, 62 °E) is post-seismic deformation from the 2013 Khash earthquake (Barnhart, Hayes, Samsonov, et al., 2014). **(f)** Applied ionospheric correction. **(g)** Applied tropospheric correction. **(h)** Applied SET correction. **(i)** Applied DEM error correction. Larger signals in the south may be bias from tropospheric residuals (Fattahi & Amelung, 2015). **(j)** Applied plate motion correction.

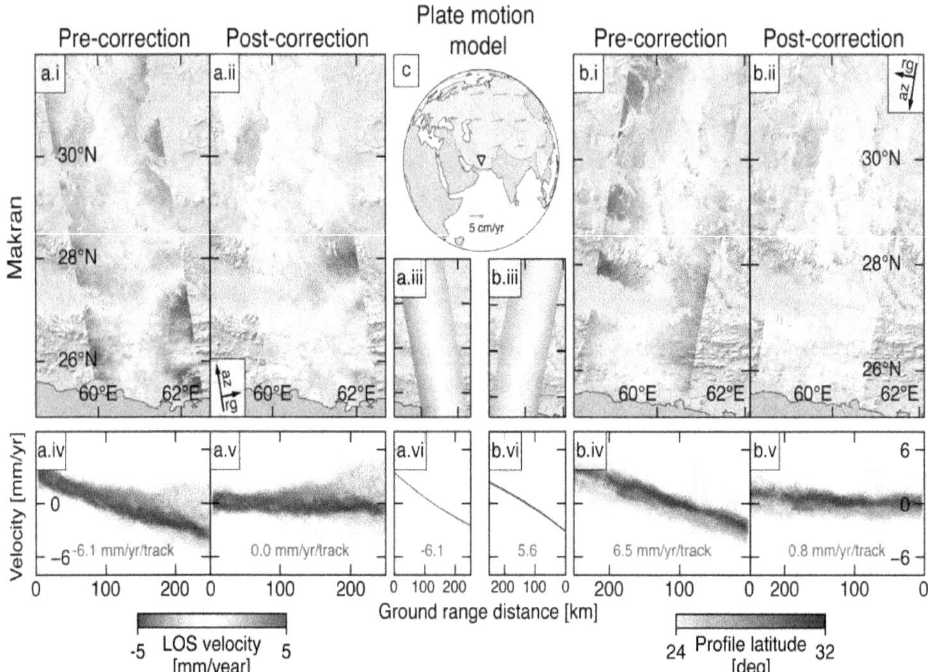

Figure 1.3: The impact of plate motion adjustments for InSAR tracks over the Makran subduction zone. For plotting purposes, we remove the median from each velocity field. (**a**) track 86 (ASC). After plate motion correction, the post-seismic signal from the 2013 Khash earthquake (Barnhart, Hayes, Samsonov, et al., 2014) can be more clearly seen in the south-east of the figure. (**b**) track 20 (DSC). (**c**) Location of tracks (a) and (b) and the velocity field of the Eurasian plate, used to correct the tracks. (**i**) Velocity before plate motion correction, but after other corrections have been applied. (**ii**) Velocity after plate motion correction. (**iii**) Applied plate motion correction. (**iv**) Across-track profile of the velocity before plate motion correction. The number below each profile is the gradient of the linear least squares fit to the profile. Note that profiles are plotted as a function of ground range, which increases with distance from the satellite. (**v**) Across-track profile of the velocity after plate motion correction. (**vi**) Across-track profile of the applied plate motion correction.

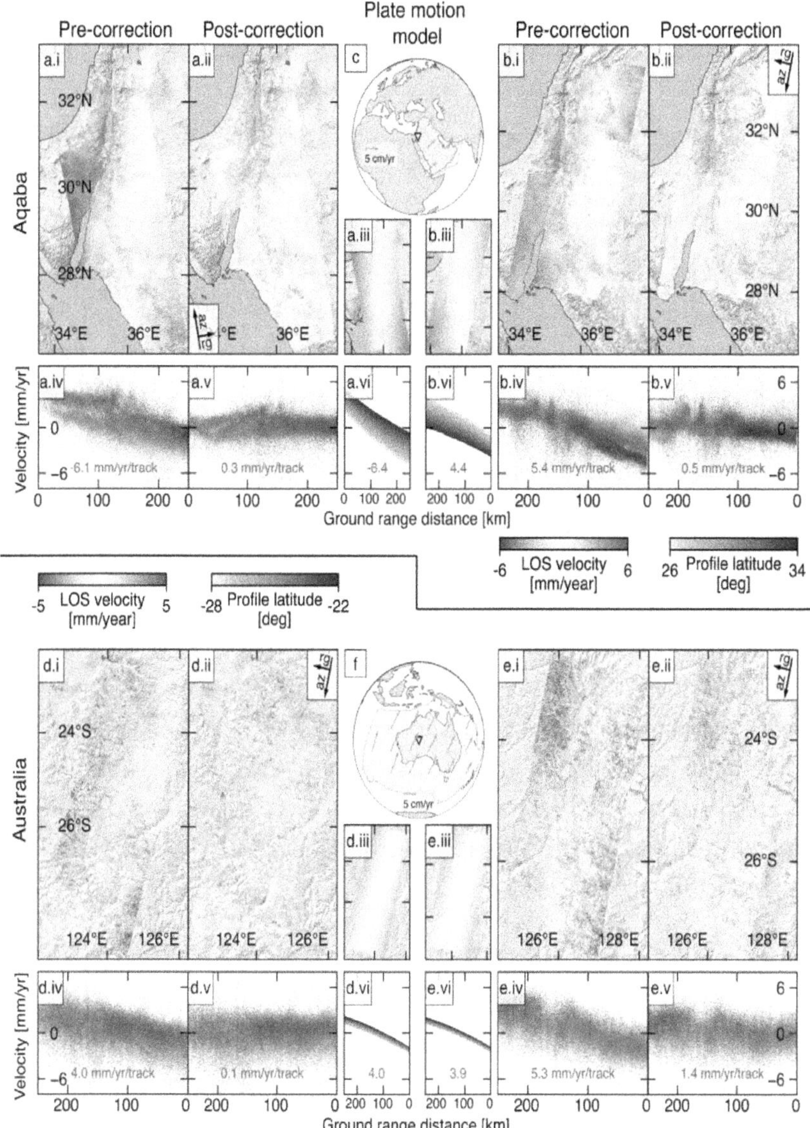

Figure 1.4: Same as Figure 1.3, but showing the tracks for the Gulf of Aqaba and Australia. (**a**) Gulf of Aqaba, track 87 (ASC). (**b**) Gulf of Aqaba, track 21 (DSC). (**c**) Location of tracks (a) and (b) and the velocity field of the Arabian plate, used to correct the tracks. (**d**) Australia, track 119 (DSC). (**e**) Australia, track 46 (DSC). (**f**) Location of tracks (d) and (e) and the velocity field of the Australian plate, used to correct the tracks. (**i**)-(**vi**) are as described in Figure 1.3.

After adjusting for plate motion, remaining long-wavelength signals could be due to the incomplete removal of some signals (predominantly the troposphere (Fattahi & Amelung, 2015; Parizzi et al., 2021)), sources that we have not corrected for (e.g., ocean tidal loading (Dicaprio et al., 2008) and orbital errors (Fattahi & Amelung, 2014)), or actual strain accumulation in the lithosphere—the signal that InSAR measurements often target. See Section A.3 for more details on the contributors to long-wavelength residuals.

Deficiencies in the plate motion model, or motion of the InSAR track reference point relative to the assumed plate, could also create long-wavelength residuals. Motion relative to the plate will be of particular importance in areas of diffuse plate boundary deformation, where it is not possible to choose a reference point that is stable with respect to the rigid plate. This could be the case for tracks covering the Makran subduction zone and the Gulf of Aqaba, both of which span plate boundary zones. In these situations, plate motion models may not fully account for the impacts of bulk motion, and using local GNSS measurements to put InSAR measurements into a local terrestrial reference frame could be necessary (Bähr, 2013).

These results emphasise the importance of accounting for the reference frame before interpreting long-wavelength InSAR-derived velocity fields. When using InSAR for studies of tectonic deformation, the most natural reference frame is one that is fixed to a stable region within the scene, so that we can interpret velocity gradients in terms of tectonic strain rather than strain-free translation and rotation. There are several situations in which failing to account for the reference frame could bias the results:

1. Combining multiple tracks to estimate 3D deformation (Fialko et al., 2001; Wright et al., 2004). In Section A.5 and Figure A.7, we show how plate motion can bias estimates of the 3D velocity field when we use an overlapping ascending and descending track to calculate horizontal and vertical velocities.

2. Modeling InSAR signals. If the long-wavelength signals in an InSAR velocity field are being modeled, and the model is assumed to not be rotating or translating, then a velocity ramp from plate motion may be modeled as strain accumulation and bias the results (e.g., changing the locking depth in a subduction zone model).

3. Comparisons between GNSS and InSAR. Both data sets must be in the same reference frame (Parizzi et al., 2020). If the GNSS are in a local reference

frame, the InSAR and GNSS velocities will diverge at long wavelengths due to the signal of plate motion in the InSAR.

Studies which removed ramps from InSAR-derived velocities to account for orbital errors may have inadvertently removed the impact of plate motion in their observations as well, reducing the biases we outlined above.

In this work, our primary focus is on the impact of horizontal plate motions, and we have not considered the contribution of long-wavelength vertical velocities. Horizontal plate motions in ITRF are generally at the scale of centimeters per year (Altamimi et al., 2017), with long-wavelength vertical motions, for example due to post-glacial rebound, significantly smaller at millimeters per year (e.g., Lau et al. (2020) and Riddell et al. (2020)). If an InSAR track is taken within a region that is experiencing constant vertical motion, this motion will also create a velocity ramp in the satellite LOS velocity field, but with ASC and DSC tracks having opposite gradients (Figure 1.1(c)). However, the amplitude of vertical velocities will result in smaller velocity gradients across the satellite track than those caused by horizontal motion (Section A.4, Figure A.6).

1.6 Conclusions

We have illustrated how InSAR velocity measurements are sensitive to tectonic plate motion in the satellite reference frame. This motion will induce ramps in the InSAR velocity fields, predominantly in the satellite range direction, of up to several millimeters per year. In all of our multi-year time series, plate motion was the dominant long-wavelength signal after ionospheric and tropospheric corrections were applied. We have presented a simple adjustment method, which uses plate motion models to remove the plate motion signal from the InSAR velocity field. This adjustment substantially reduces long-wavelength ramps in multiple InSAR tracks from three different regions of the Earth. Routinely accounting for plate motion in InSAR could reduce biases when constraining long-wavelength tectonic strain induced by local geophysical phenomena. This adjustment is likely to be particularly useful where GNSS is not available to constrain the long-wavelength deformation. The signal of plate motion in InSAR data could also be used to improve plate motion models, which may be helpful where GNSS observations are sparse but high-quality InSAR data are available.

Chapter 2

IMAGING THE MAKRAN SUBDUCTION ZONE WITH DENSE INSAR TIME SERIES

2.1 Introduction

Interferometric synthetic aperture radar (InSAR) is increasingly being used to measure small deformation signals over wide areas, generally with the aid of the Global Navigation Satellite Systems (GNSS), such as the Global Positioning System (GPS), to help constrain the long-wavelength deformation (e.g., Weiss et al. (2020) and X. Xu et al. (2021), and see Chapter 1). There are many obfuscating contributors to InSAR observations that must be accounted for in order to maximize our ability to discern long-wavelength, small-amplitude deformation without introducing GNSS. The improvements in InSAR correction methods, including corrections for plate motion we presented in Chapter 1, as well as the dramatic increase in the amount of data available in the last five years, give us the opportunity to test the ability of InSAR alone to constrain very long-wavelength deformation.

In this chapter, we test the ability of temporally-dense InSAR time series to constrain deformation in the Makran subduction zone, an enigmatic megathrust that is one of the least studied on the planet. The Makran subduction zone accommodates motion of the Arabian plate under the Eurasian plate at a rate of about 3 cm/yr, over a 1000 km long fault along the southern coasts of Iran and Pakistan. Above the megathrust lies a large accretionary prism, the sub-aerial portion of which is one of the largest in the world (Fruehn et al., 1997). To the east, the subduction zone is bounded by the left-lateral Chaman-Ornach-Nal fault, accommodating motion between the Indian and Eurasian plates, while in the west the Minab-Zendan-Palami fault zone marks the transition region between the subduction zone and the Zagros collision belt (Figure 2.1, and see Nemati (2019)).

The eastern end of the subduction zone has hosted several large events, including in 1765, 1851, and most recently a M_w 8.1 earthquake and associated tsunami in 1945 (Byrne et al., 1992). The number of casualties for this event is often cited as 4000; however, this number is based on early estimates, with later numbers closer to 300 (Hoffmann et al., 2013). Based on historic seismicity, the subduction zone seems to be bifurcated, with large ruptures limited to the eastern end and no major ruptures conclusively attributed to the western end of the subduction zone in historical records (Byrne et al., 1992; Musson, 2009). However, paleotsunami evidence suggests that the western Makran may have hosted significant earthquakes, including in 1008 and 1542 (e.g., Hoffmann et al. (2020), Prizomwala et al. (2018), Rajendran et al. (2021), and Shah-hosseini et al. (2011)).

Previous efforts using geodesy to constrain potential coupling on the megathrust include use of GNSS (Frohling & Szeliga, 2016; Khorrami et al., 2019; Penney et al., 2017) and InSAR (Lin et al., 2015). These studies generally find significant coupling on the megathrust at both the eastern and western ends, albeit with substantial uncertainty due to the limited availability of geodetic data. Results from thermal modeling of the subduction zone have also indicated the potential for a wide seismogenic zone (Khaledzadeh & Ghods, 2022; Smith et al., 2013). These studies combine a calculated temperature distribution with assumptions about the temperature range over which subduction zones are seismogenic to infer that the Makran could host earthquakes as large as M_w 9 for ruptures along the entire length of the fault. Such earthquakes, and associated tsunamis, present a substantial danger to the growing population bordering the Arabian sea (e.g., (Qiu et al., 2022; Salah et al., 2021). It is therefore important to better understand the behavior of the megathrust and constrain the potential size of future ruptures.

In our work, we used data from the European Space Agency's Sentinel-1 satellites to study an area of nearly one million square kilometers over the Makran subduction zone. We use images from six ascending and six descending tracks, totalling over 2000 acquisitions and spanning 7.5 years (from October 2014 to April 2022) to examine the ability of InSAR data to measure deformation over wide areas, without the aid of GNSS. We apply corrections, including for the ionosphere, troposphere, solid Earth tides, DEM error and plate motion, and show their importance for observing small signals over long wavelengths.

The resulting InSAR-derived velocity field allows us to observe numerous deformation processes, including post-seismic deformation in the accretionary prism from the 2013 M_w 6.1 Minab and M_w 7.7 Balochistan earthquakes (Avouac et al., 2014; Jolivet, Duputel, et al., 2014; Penney et al., 2015), and post-seismic deformation from the 2013 M_w 7.7 Khash earthquake, an intraslab earthquake that occurred at 80 km depth (Barnhart, Hayes, Briggs, et al., 2014). We also measure creep and co-seismic offsets along the Chaman fault (Dalaison et al., 2021) and rapid subsidence due to aquifer depletion (Motagh et al., 2017).

The use of ascending and descending tracks provides two components of the deformation field improving our ability to discern signals of locking on the megathrust. Post-seismic deformation at the eastern end of the subduction zone, and high tropospheric noise, do not allow us to unambiguously resolve such a signal. However, by comparing our velocity measurements with simple forward models, we can place limits on the degree of coupling on the fault. Our results suggest that scenarios where the western end of the megathrust is strongly coupled north of the coast are unlikely to be consistent with InSAR observations, under the assumptions of our simple linear elastic forward model. Coupling may therefore be less strong than some previous studies have suggested, although further work is needed to robustly constrain coupling on the megathrust.

2.2 Data and Methods

2.2.1 Interferogram Processing

We begin with Sentinel-1 Single Look Complex (SLC) data from the Alaska Satellite Facility. We use all available data from the beginning of Sentinel-1 acquisitions in October 2014 until early April 2022, resulting in approximately 7.5 years of data in each track. We process 12 tracks in total, six ascending (ASC) and six descending (DSC) from the coast up to 32°N. The details of each track are shown in Table 2.1.

We process the SLC data using the InSAR Scientific Computing Environment (ISCE) (Fattahi, Agram, et al., 2017; Rosen et al., 2012). All tracks are processed using the topsStack processing chain. We take 5 looks in azimuth and 20 looks in range before unwrapping, but do not apply filtering. Each acquisition is used to form interferograms with the next three acquisitions, resulting in roughly 500-550 interferograms per track (although the combination of Sentinel-1 A/B pairs for track 159 allows us to form 786 interferograms). We unwrap each full interferogram (from the coast to 32°N), at once, rather than splitting the track into frames. Details of unwrapping, ionosphere corrections, azimuth misregistration estimation and phase unwrapping are as described in Chapter 1, with some modifications described below. Note that, as we use the topsStack code, we do not take account of burst discontinuities introduced by the ionosphere, as discussed in Appendix A and Liang et al. (2019).

As a brief recap, ionosphere corrections rely on the dispersive nature of the ionosphere, allowing us to form interferograms at higher and lower frequency bands and estimate the ionospheric phase screen from the difference between the two interfer-

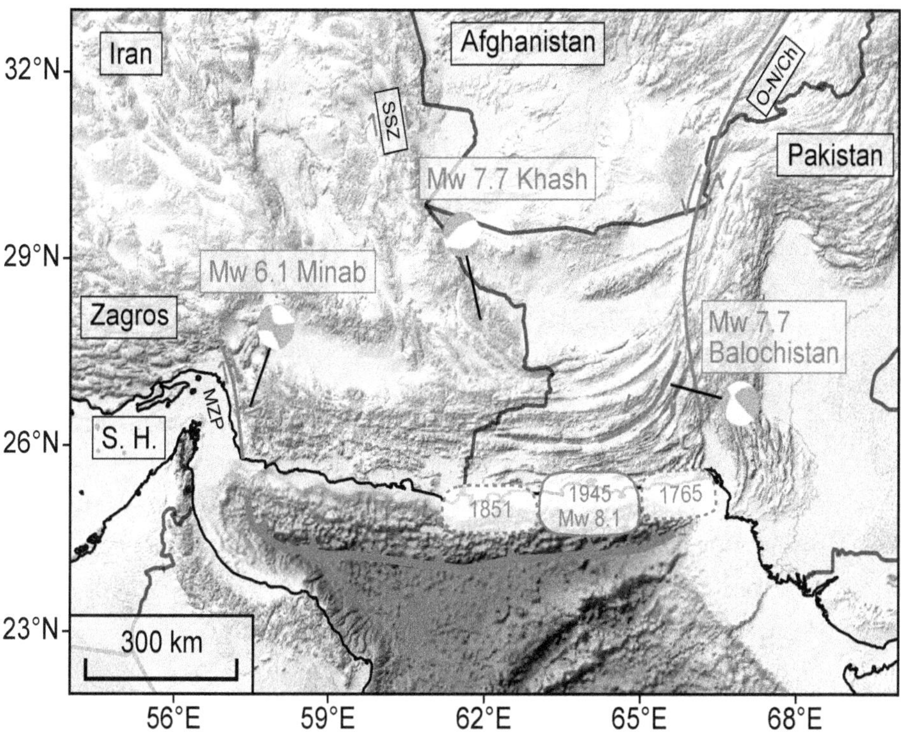

Figure 2.1: Map of the Makran region. Earthquakes and faults are shown in red, coastlines and borders are shown in black. The large red arrow at 23°N indicated the direction of convergence of the Arabian plate under the Eurasian plate used in this study. S.H.: Strait of Hormuz. MZP: Minab-Zendan-Palami fault zone. SSZ: Sistan Suture Zone. O-N/Ch: Ornach-Nal/Chaman fault zone. Approximate locations of ruptures on the megathrust in 1765, 1851, and 1945 are taken from Byrne et al. (1992). Focal mechanisms for three earthquakes in 2013 (Minab, Khash, and Balochistan) are shown, along with the rupture trace for the Hoshab fault, which hosted the Balochistan earthquake.

ograms Liang et al., 2019. Forming sub-band interferograms increases the noise in each interferogram, making it necessary to strongly filter the interferograms before unwrapping (unwrapping refers to removing the 2π phase ambiguity inherent to interferometry Chen and Zebker, 2002).

After unwrapping and calculating the ionospheric phase screen we inspect all ionosphere pairs and remove the small number of pairs that have large unwrapping errors. For tracks 57, 93, and 166, the tracks contain land on the southern side of the Strait of Hormuz. These disconnected land masses result in two areas of the ionospheric phase screen that are correctly unwrapped; however, they have an unknown offset between them as interferograms cannot be unwrapped across water. These separate areas are known as disconnected components, and can result in biases when computing the ionospheric phase that dominate the overall error budget. We therefore mask out the disconnected areas before calculating the ionosphere for these tracks.

The same ionosphere issue arises whenever we have disconnected components in the unwrapped ionospheric phase estimate (Liang et al., 2019). Such unwrapping errors can be caused by a small area of low noise (high coherence) surrounded by a narrow area of high noise (low coherence), which is in turn surrounded by high coherence (for more details on coherence, see Chapter 3). The high coherence areas unwrap individually; however, the low coherence zone between them can result in an offset between the two areas in a similar fashion to the water discussed above. Such unwrapping errors in small areas do not present significant issues for normal interferogram processing, as we can just mask out the low coherence areas and the small high coherence areas after time series processing. However, the need to strongly filter the ionosphere can cause large unwrapping errors to bleed in to adjacent areas in the ionospheric phase.

An example of how these errors affect the ionospheric velocity correction can be seen in Figure 2.2. The error here is caused by sand dunes, which have low coherence in interferograms due to their rapid change in surface properties, surrounding a small patch of higher coherence which is not connected (via higher coherence paths) to the rest of the scene. These unwrapping errors affect a significant number of our ionospheric phase estimates and result in a large error in the ionospheric correction to the InSAR velocity. In this case, the error is greater than 5 mm/yr over more than 2,500 km^2, shown in Figure 2.2(a). The size of the area affected is related to the width of the spatial filter, the extent of the low coherence area, and the size of the isolated high coherence area. For narrower filters, wider low coherence areas, and smaller high coherence areas, we would not expect to see the error extending in to the surrounding region.

Such unwrapping errors could be corrected in a similar fashion to the masking we used to address errors across the Strait of Hormuz, described above. Unfortunately, unlike with large landmasses separated by water, identifying the locations of ionosphere unwrapping errors caused by small disconnected patches of high coherence is challenging in advance of computing the ionospheric phase screen for a large number of pairs. Such corrections require processing large volumes of data, visually inspecting the processed data, and then hand-selecting the areas to be masked out before reprocessing the data, taking additional time and computational resources. In the future, automatically dealing with such unwrapping errors in the ionospheric phase screen will be important for reliable ionospheric corrections when processing large volumes of data.

Unwrapping errors affect a few specific regions of our study area, but we also find that the descending ionosphere corrections seem to add a subtle velocity ramp, with each track showing an approximately 0.5 mm/yr/track gradient in the satellite range direction. It is unclear what the origin of these ramps is; however, the fact that they appear to be very similar for every descending track suggests that they may be an artefact of the processing, and not a genuine feature of the ionosphere. For the descending tracks the expected ionospheric signal is small (e.g., Liang et al. (2019)), and as we see several errors due to unwrapping, as well as range ramps, we therefore do not apply the ionosphere corrections in the descending track for the final velocity calculations. Ascending tracks have much more substantial ionosphere, causing the actual ionospheric signal to be far greater than the errors and making ionospheric corrections necessary. The size of the ascending ionospheric signal results in it being hard to see if the ionospheric corrections have a systematic range-dependent ramp, as we see for the descending tracks. We do find one region with particularly prominent unwrapping errors at the southern end of ascending track 42, which we mask in the final velocity map. We use the temporal coherence of the ionosphere time series to define the mask, resulting in a smooth masking boundary that can be seen in the bottom right of Figure 2.11 (Yunjun et al., 2019). Other areas may also have errors due to issues with ionosphere unwrapping, although we have not systematically explored this contribution to the error budget.

Descending track 122 contains unwrapping errors in the interferogram phase related to low coherence areas around (29.7°N, 62°E). We deal with these by applying the

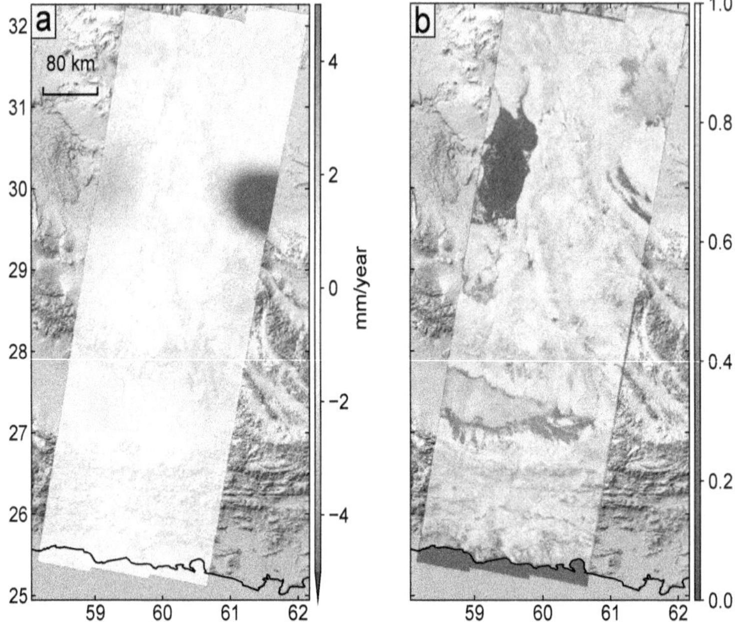

Figure 2.2: Example of errors in the ionosphere calculation **(a)** Velocity from a linear fit to the ionosphere correction time series for track 20 (descending). Note the large negative velocity around (30°N, 61.5 °E) as a result of unwrapping errors. There is also a subtle velocity ramp, of about 0.5 mm/yr, in the range direction, which is also seen in the ionosphere of other descending tracks **(b)** Average spatial coherence for all interferograms for track 20. Low coherence areas around (30°N, 61.5 °E) result in unwrapping errors which bias the ionospheric phase estimation. Filtering of the ionospheric phase then causes this error to affect surrounding areas, as can be seen in (a).

bringing unwrapping error correction method described by Yunjun et al. (2019). This method substantially reduces the number of pairs with unwrapping errors, but does not eliminate them entirely. We therefore visually inspect the interferograms and remove the remaining pairs with obvious unwrapping errors.

Ascending track 159 has a roughly year-long gap in acquisitions from March 2017 to March 2018, after which the addition of Sentinel-1B acquisitions gives a 6-day repeat period. As described by Liang et al. (2019) (Section III.F), ionospheric phase estimation for Sentinel-1 A/B pairs requires removing an empirical ramp from the phase. The error introduced by this ramp is unclear, so when we form pairs for ionospheric phase estimation we limit the number of cross A/B pairs. Specifically we form a small number of cross A/B pairs at the beginning of the Sentinel-1 B acquisitions (March 2018) and at the end (December 2021) to ensure the network is fully connected, but other than that only form A/A and A/B pairs for ionosphere estimation. We have not systematically explored how network choice affects the quality of the final ionosphere estimation.

An issue also arises when estimating the ionospheric phase for pairs of acquisitions that have different starting ranges, which can result in phase discontinuities between adjacent subswaths (Liang et al. (2019), Section III.E). These errors can be estimated and removed empirically; however, this potentially introduces additional errors into the ionospheric phase estimation. To minimise the number of pairs with different starting ranges used in the processing, we exclude any groups of acquisitions with the same starting range that have fewer than 10 acquisitions before forming interferogram networks.

2.2.2 Time Series Processing

Time series processing is also as described in Chapter 1 (using the SBAS methodology (Berardino et al., 2002), implemented in MintPy (Yunjun et al., 2019)), with one modification to deal with outliers, described below. After inverting the interferogram network and applying ionosphere, troposphere and solid Earth tides corrections in the temporal domain, we fit a linear function to the time series and calculate the root mean square of the residuals, using a temporal coherence threshold of 0.7 to mask unreliable pixels (Yunjun et al., 2019). (Unless otherwise stated, a temporal coherence threshold of 0.7 is used for masking in all velocity maps). We then compute the median absolute deviations (MAD) of the residual RMS as described in Yunjun et al. (2019), and exclude dates that have an RMS value of more than 2 MAD when estimating the DEM error (Fattahi & Amelung, 2013). This approach results in less bias from large residual tropospheric signals in the estimation of the DEM error. When estimating the final linear velocity, after removing the DEM error, we similarly exclude 2 MAD outliers to reduce the bias from the noisiest scenes.

All processing up to this point is performed in radar coordinates. After calculating the linear velocity for each track, we geocode the velocity on to a grid of 0.007 by 0.007 degrees, resulting in pixel sizes of approximately 780 meters in the latitude direction, and a variable width in the longitude direction, from 710 meters at 24°N to 660 meters as 32°N. This additional averaging reduces spatial decorrelation noise.

We then apply the plate motion correction in the geocoded domain, as described in Chapter 1. For plate motion removal we use the Eurasian plate from the ITRF2014 plate motion model (Altamimi et al., 2017).

After applying all corrections we combine the velocity fields of adjacent tracks by calculating an offset between the means of the overlap between the tracks, similar to the approach taken by Fattahi and Amelung (2016). Note that this approach ignores the difference in the satellite line-of-sight (LOS) vector in the overlapping region (Shirzaei, 2015). As we will show in Section 2.3.2, this approach to merging will create substantial biases in the final velocity field when we do not account for plate motion.

We perform the merging separately for ascending and descending tracks. We then take profiles through the merged ascending and descending track velocity fields. When taking profiles we mask out any point that is not correctly unwrapped in every interferogram (i.e., areas identified as unreliably unwrapped by the SNAPHU algorithm (Chen & Zebker, 2002)). This masking approach removes pixels where coherence is more variable, particularly areas covered by sand or agriculture, and is more aggressive than a temporal coherence threshold of 0.7. Using this mask allows us to focus on the more reliable pixels, at the expense of losing some spatial coverage.

As well as calculating a velocity from our InSAR time series, we also wish to estimate the uncertainty of this velocity. Under the assumption that residuals are uncorrelated in time and normally distributed, the velocity uncertainty for each pixel is the standard error of linear regression (e.g., Equation 10 of Fattahi and Amelung (2015)):

$$\sigma_v = \sqrt{\frac{\sum_{i=1}^{N}(d_i - \hat{d}_i)^2}{(N-2)\sum_{i=1}^{N}(t_i - \bar{t})^2}}, \tag{2.1}$$

where N is the number of acquisitions used in the linear regression, d_i is the InSAR observation at epoch i, $\hat{d}_i$ is the predicted value at i from the linear fit, t_i is the time at i and $\bar{t}$ is the mean of all t_i values. This quantity does not capture the uncertainty due to temporally correlated noise, or systematic biases in the time series (Fattahi & Amelung, 2015). It also does not give us the covariance between different pixels, although we would expect residual troposphere to lead to a spatial covariance in the velocity field (e.g., Lohman and Simons (2005)).

Table 2.1: Summary of Sentinel-1 SAR Data used. ASC: Ascending track. DSC: Descending track. Aqn. no.: Number of acquisitions used for interferogram formation. Excl. no.: Number of acquisitions excluded using the 2 median absolute deviation threshold for velocity calculation. All tracks use Sentinel-1A acquisitions apart from track 159, which combines 1A and 1B. Tracks are listed from west to east. Each track is 250 km wide and adjacent tracks have a roughly 50 km overlap.

Track	Direction	Start date	End date	Aqn. no.	Excl. no.
57	ASC	20141021	20220325	185	55
159	ASC	20141016	20220401	264	69
86	ASC	20141023	20220327	188	54
13	ASC	20141123	20220322	186	48
115	ASC	20141025	20220329	188	56
42	ASC	20141008	20220324	188	62
166	DSC	20141029	20220402	173	41
93	DSC	20141012	20220328	177	38
20	DSC	20141007	20220323	181	43
122	DSC	20141014	20220330	183	51
49	DSC	20141021	20220325	178	48
151	DSC	20141016	20220401	174	49

2.2.3 Forward Modeling

To compare our InSAR results with possible signals from coupling on the subduction megathrust, we construct simple forward models of the subduction zone and use different coupling distributions to predict the surface velocities that would be observed by the ascending and descending satellites. These velocities can then be compared to the InSAR observations. Given the uncertainties in our data, and small size of the potential signal, we do not invert for a coupling distribution in this work.

We us the megathrust geometry from Slab2 (Hayes et al., 2018) and discretize the fault into 504 triangular patches (Figure 2.3). For the shallowest part of the fault we make an approximation as to how the fault comes to the sea floor. As this area is more than 80 km from the coast, our onshore deformation predictions are not sensitive to the assumptions that we make here. We use the backslip technique of Savage (1983) and equations of Okada (1985) to model the surface deformation due to coupling on the megathrust embedded in a linear elastic half space, implemented in the Classic Slip Inversion software package (https://github.com/jolivetr/csi, Jolivet et al. (2015)). We set a convergence rate of 30 mm/yr at an angle of 10°, the same as the values used by Lin et al. (2015). The coupling value is defined as $1 - v_{patch}/v_{plate}$, where v_{patch} is the creep rate of the fault patch and v_{plate} is the

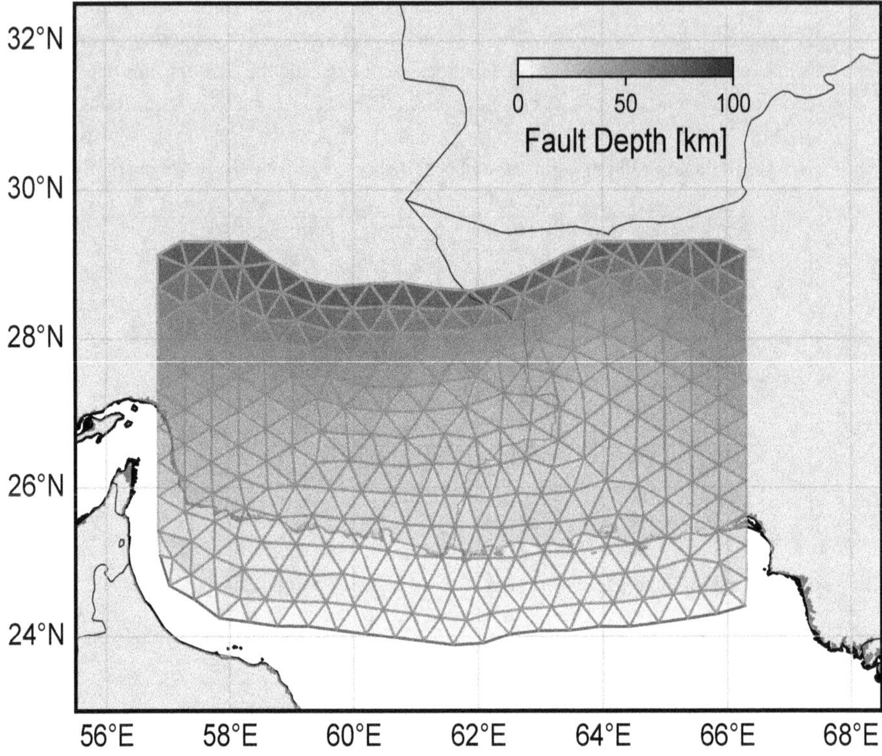

Figure 2.3: Megathrust geometry used in our forward models. The geometry is taken from Slab2 (Hayes et al., 2018), and we discretize the fault into 504 triangular patches. Black lines indicate coastlines and borders.

convergence velocity of the place (i.e 30 mm/yr). A coupling value of 1 means that the fault is fully locked, with elastic deformation accumulating at the convergence rate, while a value of 0 means the fault is sliding without accumulating strain. For a given coupling distribution we project the modeled 3-D velocity field into the ascending and descending line of sight, and then compare the prediction with the InSAR observations.

In this work we present results from two end member coupling distributions: low coupling, where the fault starts at a coupling value of 0.5 at 13 km depth and is fully decoupled below 20 km, and high coupling, where the fault is fully coupled to a depth of 30 km, transitioning to decoupled below 40 km depth. These distributions are illustrated in Figures 2.4 and 2.5, respectively. In both cases we assume that

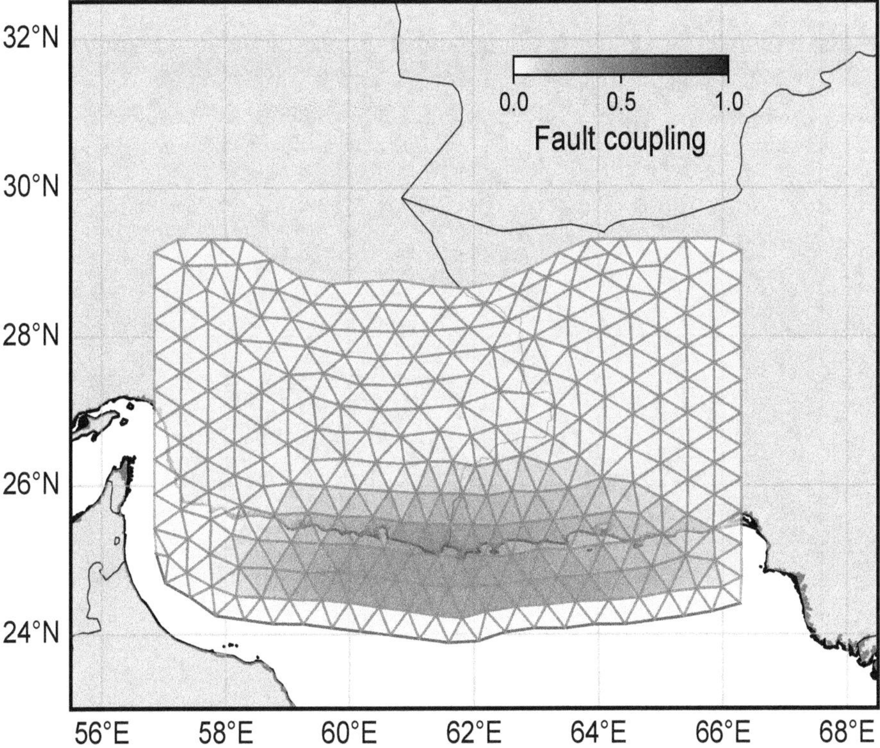

Figure 2.4: Low coupling model. The shallowest patches are all assumed to be decoupled, although this makes minimal difference to the modeled on-shore deformation. Coupling is 0.5 at 13 km depth, then transitions linearly with depth to decoupled below 20 km. Profiles of the modeled velocities at 60°E are shown in Figure 2.19

fault patches that come to the surface have zero coupling, but this assumption has minimal impact on our predicted velocities on the land.

2.3 Results

2.3.1 The Impact of Time Series Corrections

In Chapter 1, we illustrated the impact of each stage of the corrections on the long-wavelength InSAR-derived velocity fields. We apply the same corrections in this chapter, but also remove outliers before calculating the velocity. In Figures 2.7 and 2.8, we show the cumulative impact of corrections for an ascending and descending

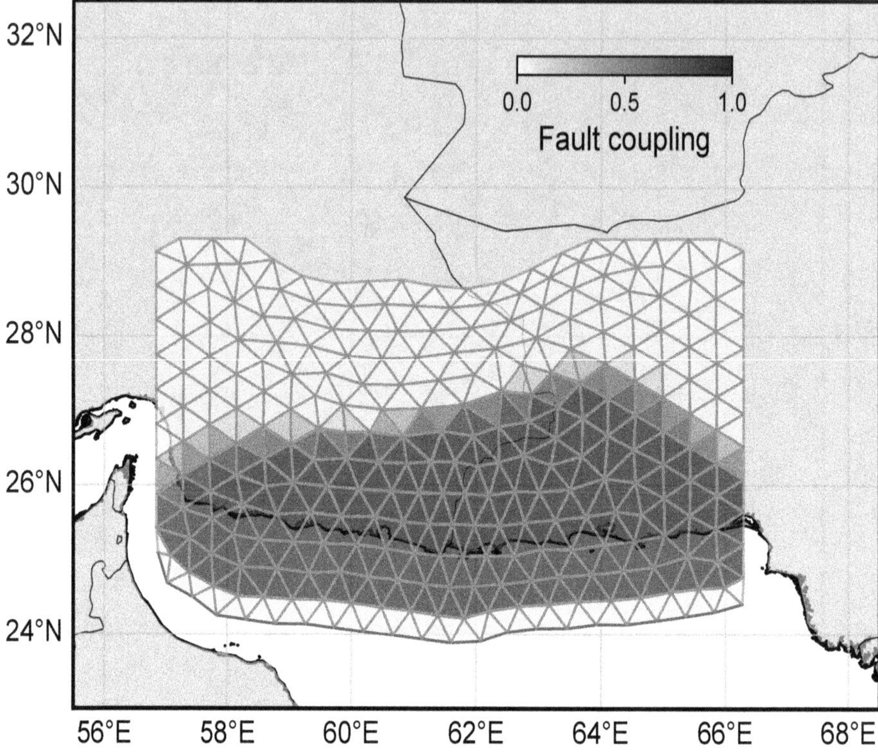

Figure 2.5: High coupling model. The shallowest patches are all assumed to be decoupled, although this makes minimal difference to the on-shore deformation. The fault is fully coupled to 30 km depth, then transitions linearly with depth to decoupled below 40 km. Profiles at 60°E are shown in Figure 2.20.

track on InSAR time series near the Makran coast, relative to a point 667 km to the north.

The initial time series shows scatter of tens of centimeters for both ascending and descending tracks, with the ascending track having much greater noise at the beginning of the time series due to ionosphere activity. Ionospheric corrections substantially reduce the variance and secular trend in the time series for the ascending track, while making a much smaller difference for the descending track. Troposphere corrections, using the ERA5 weather model, reduce the time series variance for both ascending and descending tracks. The solid Earth tide correction also reduces the variance; however, it has very little impact on the overall secular trend in the time series. The DEM error correction has the least impact on the time series.

After the above corrections have been applied, the signal of plate motion is still present in the time series (recall that we correct for plate motion in the velocity domain, rather than correcting the time series). This signal can be seen by examining the linear trend for tracks 86 and 20, shown in Figures 2.18(g) and (h) respectively. As the two tracks have opposite orbital directions, the change in satellite range between the reference point and time series location is positive for track 20 and negative for track 86, resulting in the relative LOS plate motion velocity being opposite for each track.

The final time series still show substantial scatter (e.g., around 10 cm for the ascending track in Figure 2.18(g), and somewhat less for the descending track in Figure 2.18(h)), likely due to residual troposphere (e.g., Parizzi et al. (2021)). Fattahi and Amelung (2015) showed that tropospheric noise in the region varies seasonally, and is particularly large near the coast, consistent with our results. We find sharp tropospheric fronts in our time series, particularly affecting the summer acquisitions, likely associated with the seasonal monsoon (Figure 2.6). Sharp changes in the troposphere are not well corrected by tropospheric models, and the residual tropospheric noise results in the coastal areas having the highest velocity uncertainties (Figures 2.12 and 2.14). There is a noticeable difference between the velocity uncertainties calculated for the ascending (Figures 2.12) and descending (Figures 2.14) tracks. We attribute this difference to a more energetic troposphere for the dusk-acquired ascending tracks compared to the dawn-acquired descending tracks.

To reduce the influence of large residual tropospheric signals we exclude outliers in the time series fit (Section 2.2.2). Our outlier threshold is aggressive, rejecting over 20 percent of the data for each track (Table 2.1). The changes in velocity due to outlier removal can be as high as +/- 2 mm/yr, illustrating the substantial uncertainties, predominantly due to tropospheric residuals.

2.3.2 Plate Motion and Merging Tracks

After applying all time series corrections (but not correcting for plate motion), we calculate the linear velocity and merge the tracks as described in Section 2.2.2. We show the results of this merging for the ascending tracks in Figure 2.9 and descending tracks in Figure 2.10. The across-track ramp induced by plate motion combines to create a ramp in the range direction of around 30 mm/yr over 1200 km.

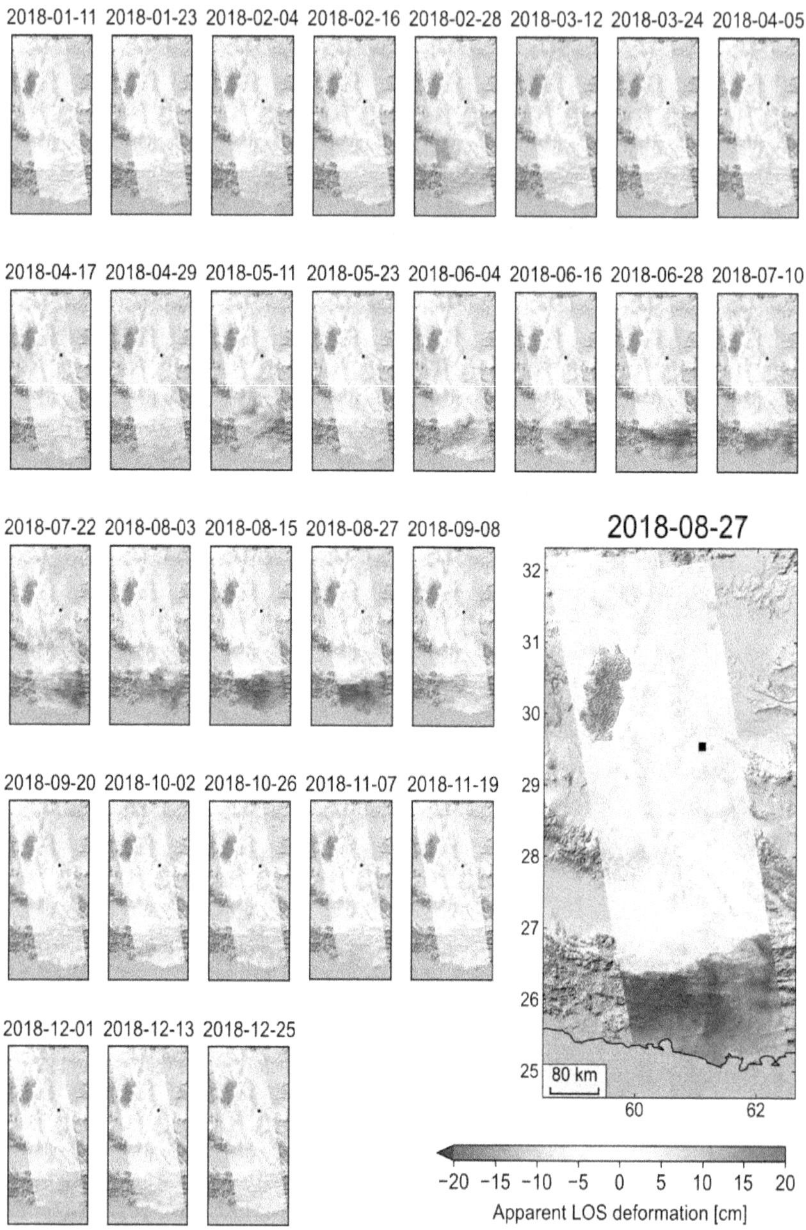

Figure 2.6: Example of strong tropospheric fronts in the InSAR time series. All 2018 data from track 86 (asc) is shown, after ionosphere corrections but before other corrections have been applied. The first date (2018-01-11) is taken as the temporal reference, and the black point shows the spatial reference. Sharp tropospheric fronts can be seen between July and August. The large inset on the bottom right highlights a particularly strong front on 2018-08-27, with over 20 cm of apparent deformation over a few kilometers.

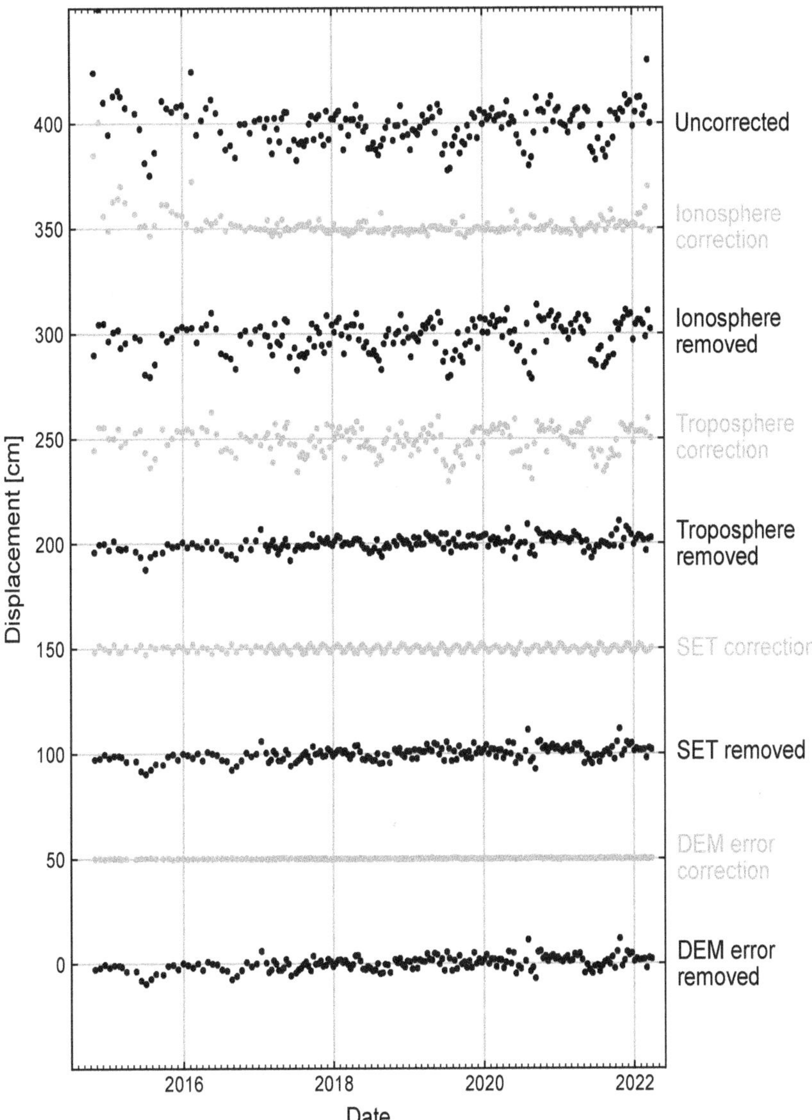

Figure 2.7: Impact of time series corrections for a point at (26°N, 60°E) relative to (32°N 60°E) for track 86a. Correction time series (grey) are subtracted from the displacement time series (black). Each time series is offset by 50 cm for display purposes. Corrections are applied cumulatively, meaning the time series at the bottom of the plot has had all the above corrections applied. Note that we do not apply plate motion corrections in the time series domain, so the final time series includes a secular trend due to plate motion. The final time series is shown on a larger scale in Figure 2.18(g).

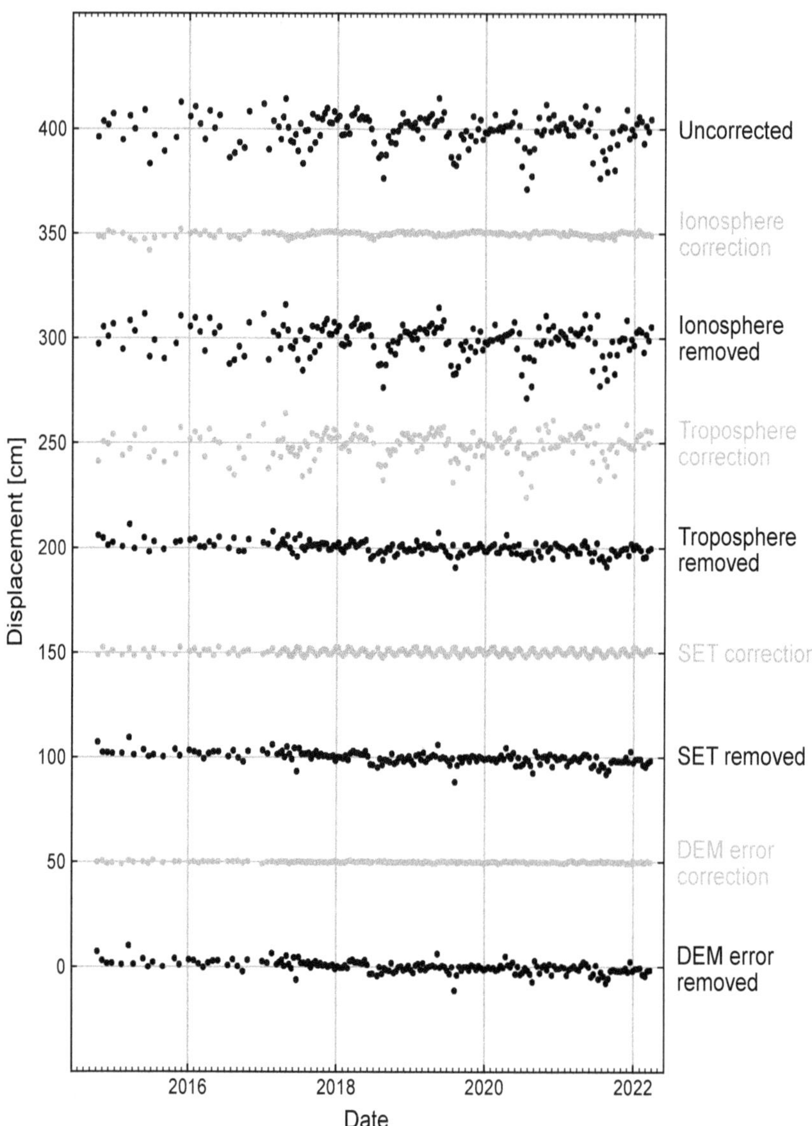

Figure 2.8: Time series corrections for track 20d. Note the much weaker ionosphere for the descending track. The final time series is shown on a larger scale in Figure 2.18(h). Caption is otherwise the same as Figure 2.7

This ramp clearly illustrates the limitations of neglecting the LOS difference in the overlap between the tracks when merging tracks without correcting for plate motion.

2.3.3 Exploring the Merged Velocity Fields

After removing the signal of plate motion from each track, we repeat the merging process and plot the results for the ascending (Figure 2.11) and descending (Figure 2.13) tracks, along with their uncertainties (Figures 2.12 and 2.14). The merged velocity fields no longer show large cross-track ramps, and allow us to discern the details of ground deformation at the level of millimeters per year over an area of nearly one million square kilometers.

There are noticeable discontinuities in the velocity between the tracks of up to several millimeters per year. These discontinuities are particularly prevalent at the southern end of the tracks. We attribute these discontinuities to two causes: (1) different noise realisations between adjacent tracks, and (2) differing sensitivities to tectonic deformation at the boundary between tracks. (1) is the likely cause of the discontinuity around (26°N, 60°E) in Figure 2.11. (2) can clearly be seen around (27°N, 64°E) in Figure 2.11, where a change of 15 degrees in the LOS incidence angle at the track boundary, coupled with predominantly westward motion from post-seismic deformation of the 2013 Balochistan earthquake (discussed below), results in a clear discontinuity of around 2 mm/yr.

We plot profiles through the velocity fields and example deformation time series in Figures 2.16 and 2.18 respectively. The locations of these profiles are illustrated in 2.15, and locations of the time series are given in Table 2.2. Figure 2.16(a) shows a profile through the ascending and descending merged velocity fields. The dominant feature is post-seismic deformation from the 2013 M_w 2013 Balochistan earthquake on the right of the profile (e.g., Jolivet, Duputel, et al. (2014), Lv et al. (2022), and Peterson et al. (2018)), which is also visible in profiles (e) and (f) and can be seen in Figures 2.11 and 2.13 as the dominant feature of the velocity field around (26-28°N,64-66°E). Ascending and descending tracks have differing sensitivities to east-west motion, resulting in different velocity profiles from the ascending and descending tracks. This post-seismic deformation has been variously attributed to after slip on the Hoshab fault combined with viscoelastic relaxation of the accretionary prism (Peterson et al., 2018), or aseismic slip on the megathrust (Lv et al., 2022). In Figures 2.18(a) and (b), we illustrate logarithmic post-seismic deformation time series from Balochistan. The comparison between these two profiles illustrates the spatial correlation of tropospheric noise (e.g., Emardson et al., 2003), with the time series showing deformation relative to a point 83 km away (Figure 2.18(a)) showing much greater scatter than deformation relative to a point 1 km away (Figure 2.18(b)).

A more subtle feature in profile 2.16(a), at 700-800 km along the profile, we attribute to post-seismic deformation from the 2013 Khash earthquake, a M_w 7.7 intraslab earthquake that occurred at 80 km depth (Barnhart, Hayes, Briggs, et al., 2014). Profile 2.16(d) gives a clearer picture of the velocity field from Khash post-seismic deformation, with a negative velocity lobe between 100 and 300 km along the profile and a positive velocity lobe between 300 and 400 km. These two lobes of the deformation can clearly be seen in Figures 2.11 and 2.13 around (28°N, 62°E). In Figure 2.18(c) we show a deformation time series from the area of peak LOS deformation in the ascending tracks. While the deformation is substantially smaller than for Balochistan post-seismic, we can see a logarithmic deformation profile with a cumulative LOS offset of 5 cm over 7.5 years.

Another region of post-seismic deformation is caused by the 2013 M_w 6.1 Minab earthquake, in the transition zone between the Makran subduction zone and the Zagros mountains (Penney et al., 2015). In Figure 2.18(d) we show a LOS deformation time series across the fault. Previous modeling work has attributed this motion to after slip (Plattner et al., 2021), and not viscoelastic relaxation. The deformation seems to have stopped by about mid-2020, although the substantial tropospheric noise makes it challenging to resolve small deformations without several years of data.

In Figure 2.18(e), we show a time series of LOS deformation across the Chaman fault, an 850 km long fault running through Afghanistan and Pakistan that accommodates motion between the Eurasian and Indian plates through both aseismic creep and co-seismic deformation (Figure 2.1). The time series exhibits both behaviors, showing slow creep and a co-seismic offset from an earthquake on June 27th 2018 (Dalaison et al., 2021).

Our velocity maps show numerous areas of rapid subsidence (< -2 cm/yr). These areas are most clearly visible in the western portion of Figures 2.9 and 2.10, where they can be seen despite the presence of the plate motion ramp. Rapid subsidence is correlated with areas of agricultural land use, and previous studies have attributed this motion to aquifer depletion due to over-extraction of water (e.g., Motagh et al. (2017)). In Figure 2.18(f), we present an example deformation time series, near the

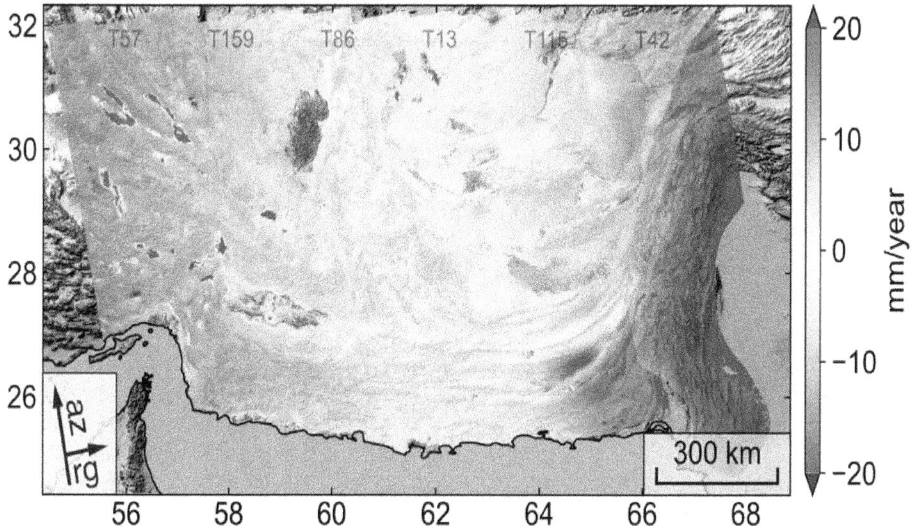

Figure 2.9: LOS velocity for ascending tracks after applying all corrections other than plate motion to every track, and merging. Plate motion creates a range-dependent velocity ramp in each track, resulting in a large ramp across the entire region. Track numbers are shown at the top of the figure. "az": azimuth direction, the satellite direction of travel. "rg": range direction, the look direction of the satellite. Positive velocities represent motion towards the satellite.

city of Rafsanjan, Iran, with a cumulative LOS offset of over 80 cm during the 7.5 year observation period.

All of our velocity maps rely on linear fits to our time series, but the data in Figure 2.18 shows deformation that is not linear in time. Behavior such as co-seismic steps and post-seismic logarithms will bias a purely linear fit. An example is the 2017 M_W 6.3 Pasani earthquake, which occurred on the eastern megathrust and caused 2-4 centimeters of vertical ground deformation (Yang et al., 2022). The linear rate around (25.5°N, 63°E) is biased by this offset. We choose a linear fit to illustrate the broad deformation trends across the region; however, a better velocity field could be calculated by modeling and removing earthquakes in the time series, and choosing different functional forms appropriate to the specific processes being studied.

2.3.4 Forward Models

To place constraints on the behavior of the subduction zone, we take four north-south profiles through our ascending and descending velocity fields, starting at the coast,

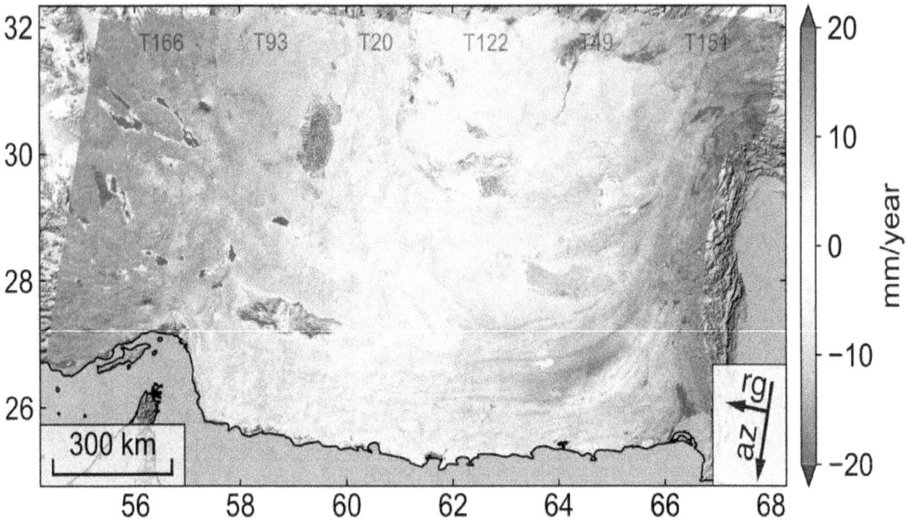

Figure 2.10: Same as Figure 2.9, except for descending tracks.

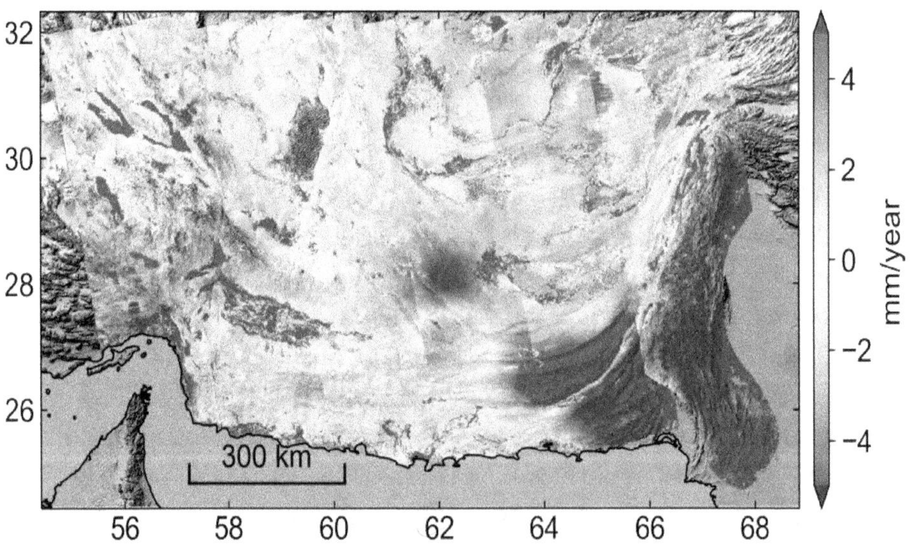

Figure 2.11: LOS velocity for ascending tracks after removing the effect of plate
motion using a plate motion model.

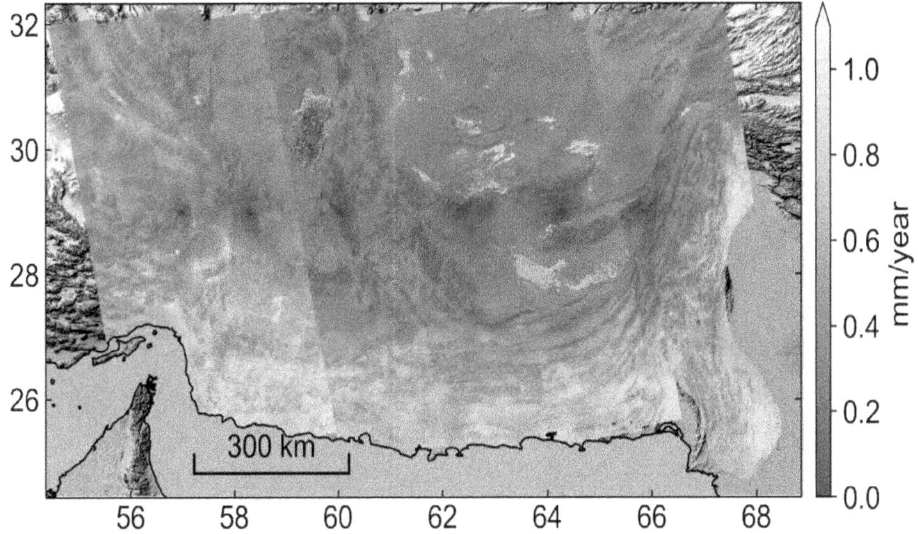

Figure 2.12: Estimated standard deviation of the time series velocity (σ_v) assuming uncorrelated Gaussian errors and after outlier removal for ascending tracks. Uncertainties are expressed relative to a reference point in each track (which has 0 uncertainty), with each reference point at a latitude of 29°N.

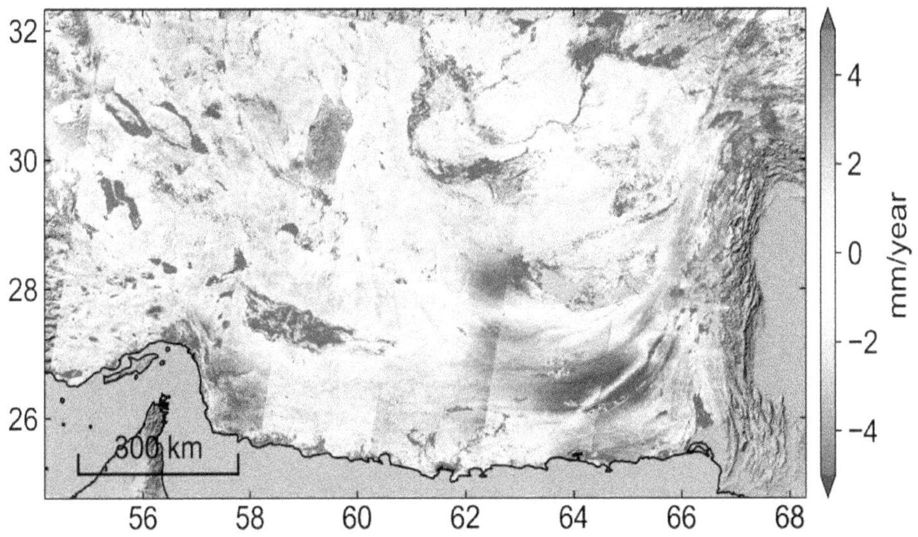

Figure 2.13: LOS velocity for descending tracks after removing the effect of plate motion using a plate motion model.

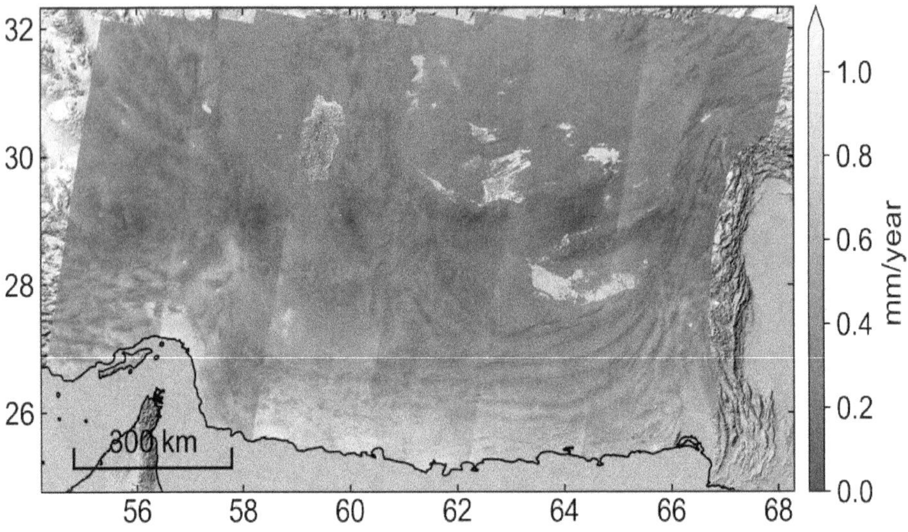

Figure 2.14: Uncertainties for the descending tracks. Caption is otherwise the same as Figure 2.12.

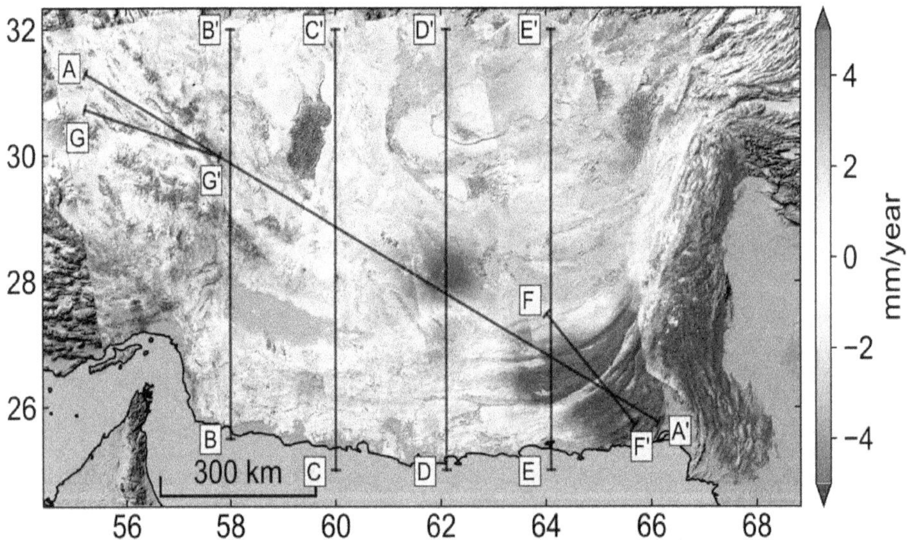

Figure 2.15: Location of the velocity profiles plotted in Figure 2.16, shown over the merged ascending track LOS velocities. Areas which do not unwrap in every interferogram have been masked, and are excluded from profiles, other than for (g), where the temporal coherence mask is used.

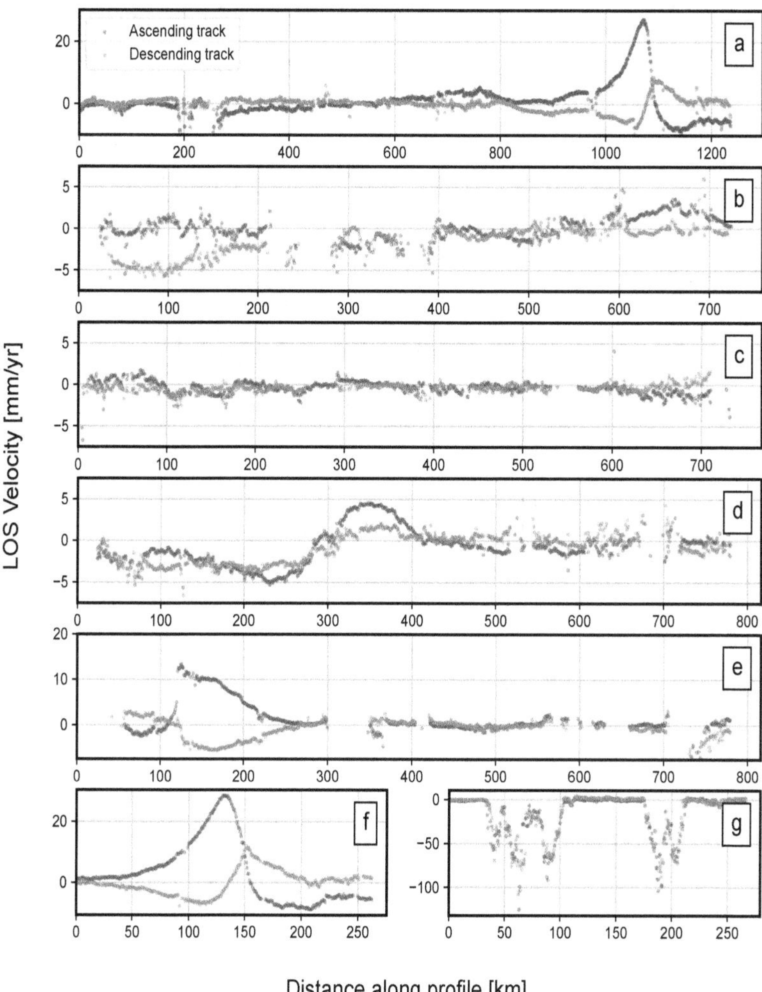

Figure 2.16: Profiles through ascending (blue) and descending (red) track LOS velocity fields. Locations of the profiles are shown in Figure 2.15, and profile distances are calculated from the letter, to the letter primed (e.g., A to A'). (a) Region-spanning profile. (b) South to north profile at 58°E (25.5°N to 32°N). (c) South to north profile at 60°E (25°N to 32°N). (d) South to north profile at 62.1°E (25°N to 32°N). The left side of the profile spans post-seismic deformation from the 2013 Khash earthquake. (e) South to north profile at 64.1°E (25°N to 32°N). The left side of the profile spans post-seismic deformation from the 2013 Balochistan earthquake. Note that profiles (b)-(e) are chosen to lie within individual tracks to avoid offsets at the track boundaries. (f) Profile spanning post-seismic deformation from the 2013 Balochistan earthquake. (g) Profile spanning rapid subsidence near the city of Rafsanjan, Iran, likely due to aquifer depletion.

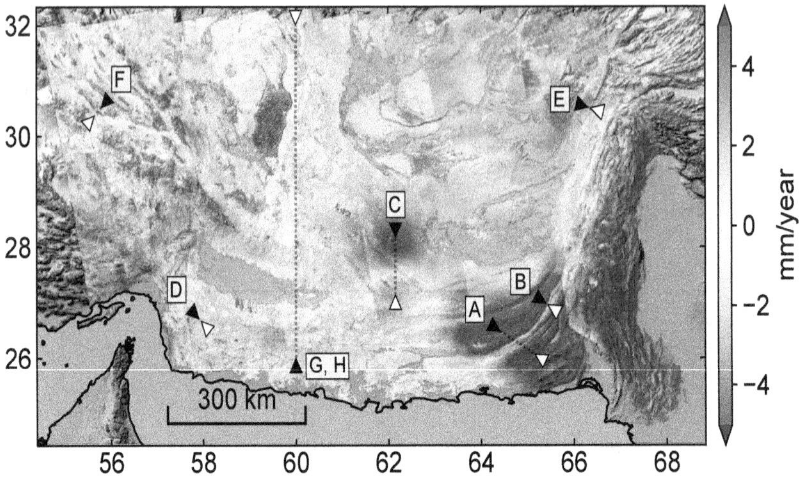

Figure 2.17: Locations of time series (a)-(h) plotted in Figure 2.18, plotted over ascending track velocities. All time series are plotted relative to a reference point. The location of the time series is shown with a black triangle, and the location of the reference point is shown with a white triangle. Note that all time series are relative to a point within the same track as the chosen point, and are plotted before the removal of the plate motion signal (which is only significant for points far from their reference, such as G and H. Tracks and exact locations are given in Table 2.2.

Letter	Name	Track	Location (°N, °E)	Reference (°N, °E)	Distance (km)
(a)	Balochistan	115a	26.47, 64.44	26.08, 65.15	83
(b)	Balochistan	115a	26.966, 65.421	26.959, 65.429	1
(c)	Khash	13a	28.16, 62.15	27.15, 62.15	112
(d)	Minab	57a	26.688, 57.928	26.67, 57.95	3
(e)	Chaman	42a	30.511, 66.325	30.50, 66.363	4
(f)	Rafsanjan	166d	30.505, 55.780	30.384, 55.655	18
(g)	Makran	86a	26.0, 60	32.0, 60.0	667
(h)	Makran	20d	26.0, 60	32.0, 60.0	667

Table 2.2: Details of the time series plotted in Figure 2.18. "Track" refers to the Sentinel-1 track, with "a" and "d" referring to ascending and descending tracks respectively. Time series are taken at the point given by "Location" and the InSAR reference point is set at "Reference." "Distance" refers to the distance between the time series location and the reference point.

which are shown in Figures 2.16(b)-(e). The locations of these profiles are chosen such that they lie entirely within a single ascending and descending track, so we do not introduce additional uncertainties related to track merging. Of these profiles,

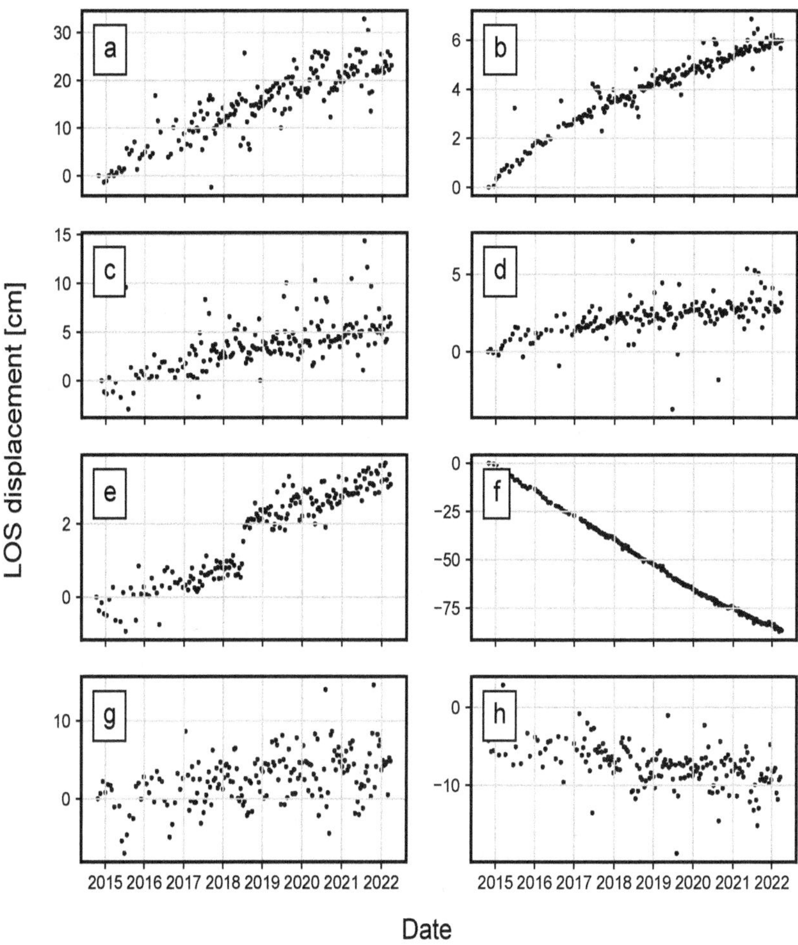

Figure 2.18: InSAR LOS displacement time series illustrating a variety of different temporal behaviors in our region. The locations of the time series and reference points are given in Figure 2.17 and Table 2.2. (a) post-seismic deformation from the 2013 Balochistan earthquake near the point of peak deformation. (b) Post-seismic deformation from the 2013 Balochistan earthquake across a portion of the fault creeping at the surface. The proximity to the reference point (1 km away) results in much lower tropospheric noise compared to (a). (c) post-seismic deformation from the 2013 Khash earthquake. (d) post-seismic deformation from the 2013 Minab earthquake. (e) Creep on the Chaman fault, and co-seismic offset from an earthquake on 2018-06-27 (Dalaison et al., 2021). (f) Rapid subsidence near the city of Rafsanjan, Iran, likely due to aquifer discharge (Motagh et al., 2017). (g) Time series near the coast for track 86 after corrections shown in Figure 2.7. A linear trend partly due to plate motion can be seen. (h) Same as (g), but for track 20, after corrections shown in Figure 2.8.

2.16(d) and (e) have substantial signals from Khash and Balochistan earthquake post-seismic signals respectively, and (b) lies in the transition zone between the Makran subduction zone and the Zagros mountains collision zone (e.g., Penney et al. (2015) and Regard et al. (2005)). We therefore cannot straightforwardly compare deformation in these profiles to different models of coupling on the megathrust. The profile (c), at 60°E, does not seem to have obvious sources of contamination, so we select this profile for comparison with forward models.

In Figures 2.19 and 2.20, we compare our velocity profiles with predicted LOS deformation rates from the two coupling models presented in Figures 2.4 and 2.5. Note that we plot these profiles in terms of distance from the subduction trench. The high sediment input means there is not a clear trench in the bathymetry (Schlüter et al., 2002), but we can still locate a deformation front, which is at around 24°N for our profile along 60°E. We add to the velocity profiles uncertainty estimates based on the calculated σ_v (Equation 2.1). For a conservative estimate of the error, we set our error range to be +/- $2\sigma_v$. This choice gives us an error range of around +/- 2 mm/yr near the coast, relative to a point around 400 km to the north.

For our simple linear elastic forward models, the transition between coupled and decoupled behavior on the megathrust corresponds to a peak in the surface velocity, with the size of that peak related to the strength of coupling and depth ranges over which that transition occurs. The assumed convergence direction of 10° means that megathrust coupling results in an eastward component of the deformation field. As a result of their differing lines of sight, ascending and descending tracks have different sensitivities to this eastward motion, making the combination of ascending and descending tracks a key tool for constraining potential coupling. This difference in sensitivity can be seen prominently in the high coupling model (Figure 2.20), where the predicted ascending and descending track LOS velocities differ by over 4 mm/yr near the coast.

The low coupling model in Figure 2.19 gives velocity predictions that lie well within the bounds of our observational uncertainty. Therefore, this coupling scenario cannot be ruled out by our data. Lower coupling scenarios, including a completely unlocked megathrust, are also possible, and coupling could be somewhat stronger, particularly off the coast where we have little sensitivity. We illustrated such an intermediate coupling model in Figure 2.21, which is at the limit of what is compatible with our data, given the conservative error bounds. For the high coupling model in Figure 2.20, the predicted velocities are clearly not consistent with the observed velocity fields, lying well outside of the observational uncertainty bounds for much of the 200 km closest to the coast. A visual inspection of the other north-south profiles in Figure 2.16 does not show any clear evidence for the kind of strong coupling north of the coast that we use in Figure 2.20, although, as previously mentioned, there are other signals present in these profiles that could hide coupling signals. These results suggest that, under the simplifying assumptions of our fault geometry, convergence velocity, and forward model, strong coupling on the megathrust is unlikely to be present north of the coastline, at least for the western part of the subduction zone. However, these results do not rule out the potential for a significant earthquake on this part of the subduction zone.

2.4 Discussion

2.4.1 Quality of the InSAR-Derived Velocity Fields

The uncertainties we presented in Figures 2.12 and 2.14 represent the estimate of the error on the velocity, relative to the reference point within the track, and under the assumption of temporally uncorrelated Gaussian errors (Fattahi & Amelung, 2015). It does not capture biases in the velocity, for example related to incomplete removal of plate motion, or errors in the offsets between the tracks used when merging. Within each track the error is likely dominated by residual tropospheric signal (e.g., see Fattahi and Amelung (2015) and Parizzi et al. (2021), and our discussion of uncertainties in Appendix A), with some small contribution from neglecting the burst discontinuities when correcting the ionosphere (Liang et al. (2019), and see Appendix A). Treating the error as uncorrelated in time is an approximation, as there is seasonal variability in the tropospheric signal (Fattahi & Amelung, 2015). Quantifying the uncertainties using the residuals from a purely linear fit is therefore potentially an overestimate of the uncertainty in the velocity.

Our InSAR velocity uncertainties are substantially larger than those found by Lin et al. (2015) (around 0.5 mm/yr, see their Figure 2(b)) for three Envisat tracks in the eastern Makran, in spite of their lack of ionosphere corrections, and much smaller quantities of data. Their use of dusk-acquired descending tracks, which are much less affected by the ionosphere, and were mostly acquired during a relative low in solar activity during the period 2006-2010 (Liang et al., 2019), means the ionosphere likely has a small effect. They also make use of direct observations of the troposphere from the Medium Resolution Imaging Spectrometer on board Envisat, which increases the accuracy of their tropospheric corrections. However, it is still surprising that their estimated errors are so much lower with no more than 23

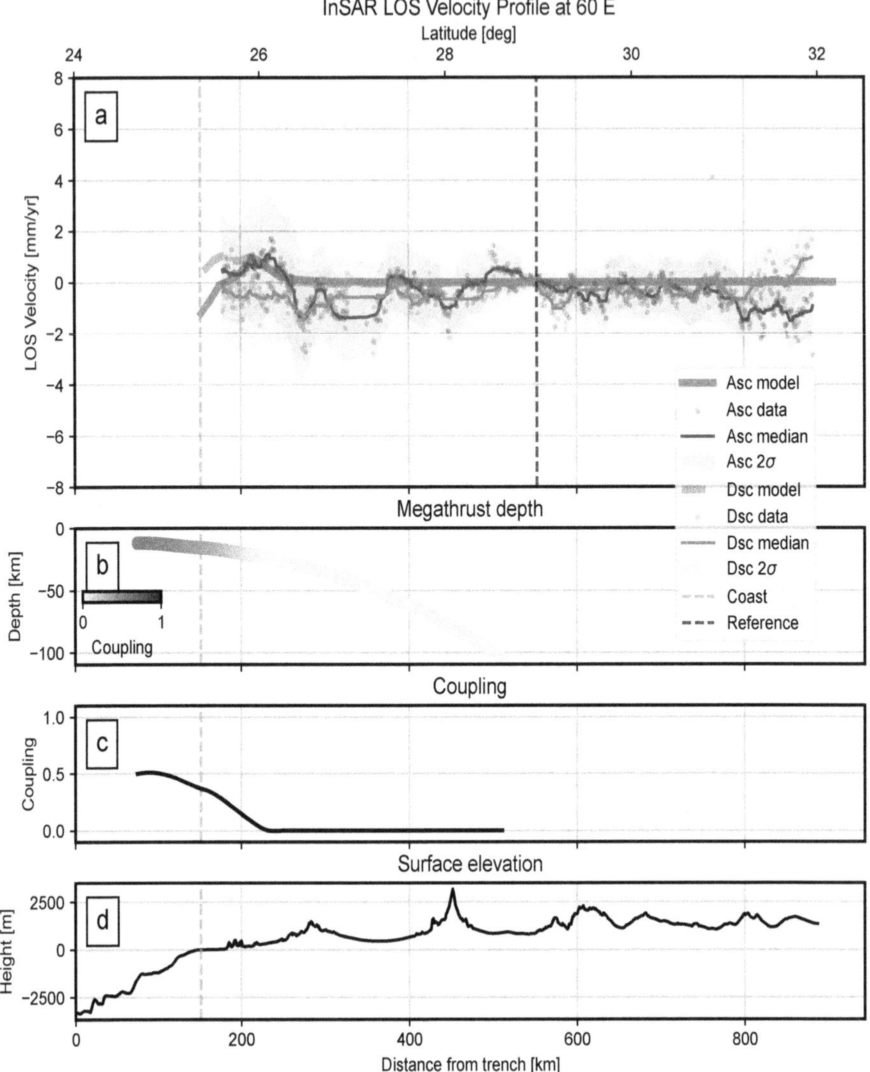

Figure 2.19: Profiles at 60°E for the low coupling model shown in Figure 2.4. (a) Profiles through the LOS velocity and estimated uncertainties ($2\sigma_v$) for ascending (asc) track 86 and descending (dsc) track 20. All velocities and uncertainties are relative to the reference point. Thin blue (asc) and red (dsc) lines show the running median of the InSAR data. Thick blue (asc) and red (dsc) lines show the predicted LOS velocity from the forward model. (b) Profile through the megathrust depth, with the color showing the coupling. (c) Plot of the coupling from (b). (d) Surface elevation profile.

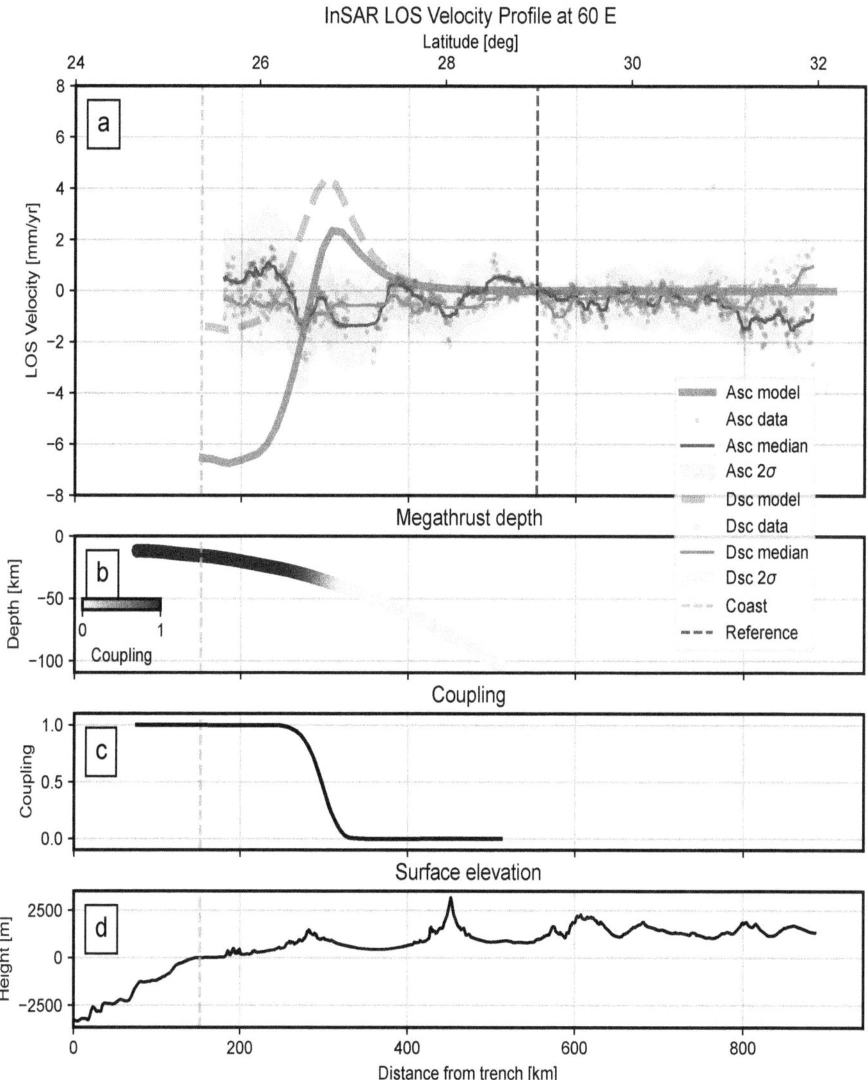

Figure 2.20: Same as Figure 2.19, but with higher coupling on the megathrust (coupling as shown in Figure 2.5). The increased coupling results in larger variations in the predicted InSAR LOS velocity, which are not consistent with our observations.

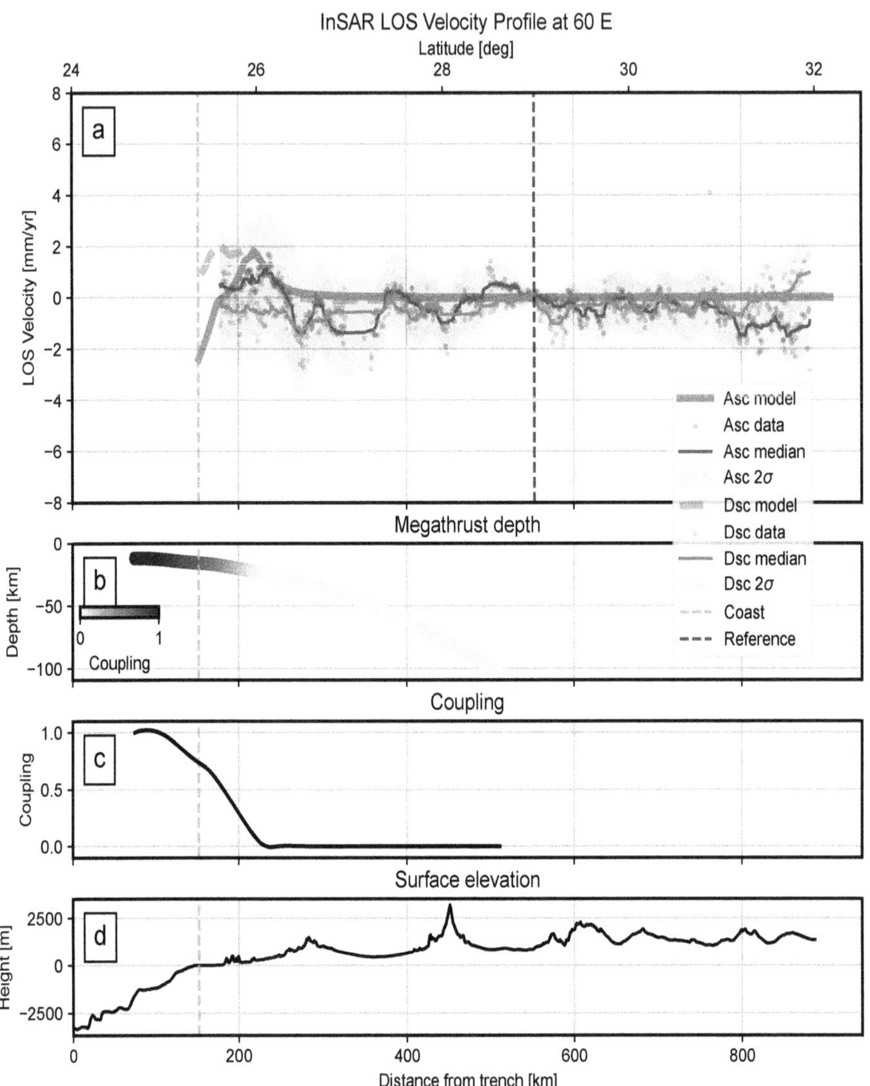

Figure 2.21: Same as Figures 2.19 and 2.20, but with intermediate coupling on the megathrust. This coupling is at the limit of what is compatible with our data, given the conservative errors bounds we have chosen.

acquisitions in a track. This comparison supports the idea that our error estimates are likely overly conservative.

Our approach of rejecting outliers and then performing an unweighted linear fit to the time series is a sub-optimal approach to extracting the velocity and its uncertainty. A more rigorous approach would be to quantify the uncertainty in each interferogram, then propagate that uncertainty through the calculation of the time series and then the velocity. This propagation of uncertainty could be done assuming that the sole contributor to the uncertainty is from residual troposphere (e.g., Parizzi et al. (2021)), or by using a full noise model for the InSAR time series (e.g., Agram and Simons (2015)). Such approaches allow for the use of all available data, with noisier acquisitions down-weighted in the calculation of the velocity, and provide a more rigorous estimate of the error on the final velocity. The Makran region presents specific challenges to such approaches, as the tropospheric signal can show sharp north-south variation. This variation means that the method of calculating a single tropospheric covariance function for the entire track will likely not give a representative uncertainty (e.g., Emardson et al. (2003) and Lohman and Simons (2005)). It may therefore still be necessary to reject acquisitions that show strong variations in tropospheric noise, or better account for this spatial variability in applying corrections and quantifying the uncertainty (e.g., Cao et al. (2021) and Murray et al. (2021)). A rigorous estimate of the data uncertainty is a key element of any probabilistic estimate of megathrust coupling, and is particularly important given the apparently small signal to noise ratio in the Makran region.

The above discussion applies to the uncertainties within individual tracks, but not the merged tracks. When merging tracks, we are attempting to take velocity fields that are expressed relative to a separate reference point within each track, and create a single velocity field that is relative to one reference point, i.e., putting all tracks into the same reference frame. With all tracks showing deformation relative to the same reference frame, we can interpret long wavelength signals across multiple tracks in terms of regional tectonics. The process of putting multiple InSAR tracks into the same reference frame is often done with the aid of GNSS (e.g., Weiss et al., 2020; X. Xu et al., 2021). While algorithms for combining multiple InSAR tracks without GNSS have been developed, they generally rely on the assumption that the LOS displacement does not vary significantly between overlapping tracks (e.g., Shirzaei (2015)).

As mentioned in Section 2.3.3, ground motion with the overlapping region between the tracks can bias the calculated offset due to the projection of that deformation into the different satellite lines of sight. This bias will then propagate as each subsequent track is merged, with the merged tracks before plate motion correction providing a clear example (Figures 2.9 and 2.13). These biases are effectively errors in reference frame estimation. Even after plate motion removal, our merged tracks contain biases in the offset estimation, for example due to the Balochistan post-seismic signal. It is hard to quantify the impact of these errors without comparison to dense GNSS stations; however, it seems reasonable that the bias could be in the range of 1-2 mm/yr from visual inspection of profiles crossing multiple tracks.

In the ideal case, if the reference region for every track is placed in a point that is stationary with respect to the overall plate, and subject to low noise, no offset between the tracks will actually be necessary, as each track will already be expressed relative to the plate and so can be directly compared. Given that we are unlikely to pick perfectly stationary and noise free reference regions, we could attempt to merge tracks by using only the overlap regions which are least affected by noise and ground deformation, which would likely reduce the biases that we see in our current merged velocity fields. Beyond approaches to merge InSAR tracks that are each relative to a separate reference, work on absolute phase change recovery in InSAR (X. Xu & Sandwell, 2020), and SAR geolocation (Cong et al., 2012; Eineder et al., 2011) may also prove useful for combining multiple SAR/InSAR tracks without the aid of GNSS.

2.4.2 Interpretation of Modeling Results

Based on comparisons between our linear elastic forward models and InSAR velocity profiles, we claim that scenarios where the fault is strongly coupled north of the coast are unlikely. The assumed convergence direction, combined with the two lines of sight from ascending and descending tracks, provide a useful tool for resolving strong coupling scenarios, as we would expect them to create resolvable differences in the ascending and descending track profiles. Given the conservative error bars we place on our velocity profiles, the coupling scenario Lin et al. (2015) presented for the eastern end of the subduction zone is possible at the western end, highlighting the importance of precise errors when measuring coupling.

There are several limitations to our model. Low seismicity and logistical challenges of working in the region have resulted in the megathrust geometry being relatively poorly constrained, and the Slab2 model does not include data from recent studies (e.g., see Priestley et al. (2022), and references therin). While the slab geometry could be wrong, if the convergence direction and assumption of linear elastic deformation are reasonable approximations, we would still expect to be able to resolve high coupling north of the coast, as it would create differences between the ascending and descending tracks on the order of several millimeters per year.

The assumption that strain is accommodated purely elastically in the accretionary wedge is clearly an approximation, as evidenced by co-seismic and post-seismic deformation from the 2013 Balochistan and Minab earthquakes. If a substantial fraction of the convergence was accommodated by permanent deformation, that would reduce the amount of stored elastic energy that could be released in an earthquake. Haghipour et al. (2012) find that 3% of the Arabian-Eurasian convergence is accommodated by internal deformation of the accretionary wedge in the Iranian Makran, suggesting that the assumption of elasticity is not unreasonable. Our model could likely be improved by the use of a layered elastic half space, as was used by Lin et al. (2015).

We use the constant convergence velocity of Lin et al. (2015) (30 mm/yr, at $10°$), based on results from DeMets et al. (2010) and Argus et al. (2010). However, this value relies on sparse GNSS stations, we would expect it to vary somewhat along the megathrust (Khorrami et al., 2019). Lin et al. (2015) explored the impact of varying the convergence direction on the fit to their data, finding that a westward component to the convergence gave a worse fit to the data at the eastern end of the subduction zone (see their supplementary Figure 8). Looking at the velocities over the coastal region of the western Makran in Figure 2.11 (around ($26°N$, $59°E$)), and the profiles in Figure 2.16, we can see areas near the coast where the ascending track velocity is larger than the descending track velocity (at 100 km in profile 2.16(b), 50 km in profile 2.16(c), and 100 km in profile 2.16(d)). Such a pattern could potentially indicate westward motion (i.e., moving away from the descending satellite, towards the ascending satellite), rather than the eastward motion predicted by our chosen convergence direction. These velocity differences are within our uncertainties, so we cannot interpret them in terms of deformation, but reducing the noise level with more data and better corrections may allow such differences between the ascending and descending tracks to be interpreted as variations in the convergence direction along strike. The overlap region between adjacent tracks of the same direction could also be used to provide an additional look angle (assuming the tracks have been merged using a non-deforming part of the overlap region).

While our work suggests that a fully coupled megathrust in the western Makran is unlikely, this does not rule out a substantial rupture. Previous computational work (Noda & Lapusta, 2013), and simulations that we present in Chapter 4, illustrate how dynamic weakening can allow ruptures to propagate through areas of faults with low coupling. We therefore caution that constraining the coupling distribution alone is not sufficient to fully rule out larger magnitude events.

2.5 Conclusions

We test the ability of InSAR to constrain deformation over wide areas after corrections for the ionosphere, troposphere, solid Earth tides and plate motion. We study the Makran subduction zone, on the Iran-Pakistan border, revealing deformation from fault creep, co-seismic and post-seismic offsets, and aquifer depletion. Our results show the importance of plate motion corrections when combining multiple tracks. One notable observation is that of ongoing post-seismic deformation from the 2013 M_w 7.7 Khash earthquake, which ruptured the subducting slab at a depth of 80 km.

Tropospheric noise and post-seismic deformation results in us being unable to resolve deformation due to coupling on the megathrust. However, by comparing our velocity measurements with simple forward models we can place constraints on the likely degree of coupling. The combination of ascending and descending tracks is particularly useful for resolving coupling signals due to the differing sensitivities to east-west motion between the tracks and the eastward component of the convergence direction between the plates. Comparisons between our models and observations suggest that the western Makran is unlikely to be strongly coupled north of the coast. However, significant uncertainties remain, and we cannot rule out the possibility of a significant earthquake in the western Makran.

Future work could focus on rigorous handling of data errors, allowing more data to be used and a reliable uncertainty on the final velocity to be derived. This uncertainty could then be used for a probabilistic inversion of coupling. More data and improved tropospheric correction methods will further help to reduce the noise. Further work is also needed on the ionospheric correction method to automatically deal with unwrapping errors when processing large volumes of data.

Chapter 3

DEEP LEARNING-BASED DAMAGE MAPPING WITH INSAR COHERENCE TIME SERIES

3.1 Introduction

In the wake of major natural disasters, emergency services need a rapid and accurate assessment of the damage over a wide area in order to quickly direct their response and estimate losses. However, damage to infrastructure and communications networks often makes prompt on-the-ground damage assessment difficult or impossible. Under these circumstances, remote sensing can either complement, or provide a useful alternative to, ground-based assessments (Voigt et al., 2016).

Assessments of damage due to a natural disaster can be obtained by comparing satellite observations from before and after the event. One approach is the use of change detection on very high resolution optical data ($\approx$ 50 cm $\times$ 50 cm pixels) (Dalla Mura et al., 2008; Pesaresi et al., 2007). However, the utility of optical images for disaster response can be hampered by the need for timely data, requiring cloud free conditions and sufficient solar illumination (Brunner et al., 2010).

Satellite-based synthetic aperture radar (SAR) is an imaging technique that offers advantages over optical data by providing images in all weather conditions, day or night (e.g., Rosen et al. (2000) and Ulaby and Long (2015)). SAR relies on active imaging using microwave (centimeter-scale) wavelengths emitted by the satellite, with the sensor recording the amplitude and phase of the reflected radar pulse to produce images at meter-scale resolution. The availability of SAR images depends only on the orbital parameters of the satellite.

Damage detection using SAR relies on separating normal changes in the radar backscatter properties of the ground (e.g., due to agricultural activities, vegetation growth, snow, rainfall, and even vehicle motion in a car park) from anomalous changes attributed to disaster-induced damage. The changes can be quantified using the coherence of the radar echo between subsequent acquisitions (Zebker and Villasenor (1992), and see Eq. 3.1). One current method of mapping damage uses a pair of SAR acquisitions just before the event and a pair of acquisitions that span the event, allowing for a comparison between the amount of ground surface change without any damage to the amount of ground surface change that occurs during the event (Yun et al., 2015). This method relies on human judgment in setting an appropriate threshold for classifying areas as damaged, usually assumed to be constant for all locations in the SAR scene, as well as for selecting suitable pre-event acquisitions (Yun et al., 2015).

There are now satellite SAR missions with revisits on a time-scale of days, and many parts of the Earth have repeat observations by the same satellite constellation going back several years. These developments allow for the possibility of using pre-event multi-year time series to separate out regularly occurring anthropogenic and natural surface changes from changes caused by a given natural disaster. These data have only recently begun to be exploited by researchers for damage mapping purposes (Jung et al., 2018; Karimzadeh et al., 2018; Washaya et al., 2018). The desire and opportunity to perform damage classification on large and complex SAR data sets motivates us to explore the use of deep learning techniques.

Deep learning relies on feeding input data through multiple layers of non-linear parameterized functions, also known as a deep learning architecture, to transform input data into desired outputs which can be used for regression or classification (3Blue1Brown, 2017; Goodfellow et al., 2016; LeCun et al., 2015). In supervised deep learning, the function parameters are optimised, during a process known as training, to minimise the misfit between the functions' output and known training data (*ground truth*). For example, in image classification, the function input is an image with a known classification (e.g., "dog," "cat," "tree," etc.), and the function outputs are the probabilities of the image having each classification, with the set of possible classifications finite and fixed. The functions' parameters are optimized to maximize the probabilities assigned to correct classifications for images in a data set, and the final resulting function can then be used to classify previously unseen images. Generally, in supervised learning, the functions are trained using data from the *training set* and then evaluated on a separate data set, the *validation set*, which is unseen during training to ensure the learned functions represent generalizable rules, rather than just a memorization of the training set.

Deep learning has proven to be an effective way to extract insights from large data sets with little or no assumptions about the underlying data, and minimal human intervention (LeCun et al., 2015). The growing body of available satellite data has prompted recent work to combine satellite data with deep learning techniques to study volcanoes (Anantrasirichai et al., 2019), fires (Kong et al., 2018) and flooding (Y. Li et al., 2019) among other examples.

Recurrent neural networks (RNNs) are a type of deep learning architecture particularly well suited to dealing with sequential (e.g., time-ordered) data (Lipton et al., 2015; Olah, 2015). RNNs have been applied to a wide range of tasks, from predicting the next character in a word (Sutskever et al., 2014) to precipitation forecasting (Shi et al., 2015) and seismic phase association (Ross, Yue, et al., 2019). By training an RNN on a large number of previously observed time series, the network can be used to classify new time series observations and to forecast future time steps. When using an RNN for time series forecasting, the deviation between forecast values and observations can be used for anomaly detection (Malhotra et al., 2015).

The ability of RNNs to learn generalized rules from large time series data sets makes them a good candidate for application to large satellite time series observations, and RNNs have recently begun to be used on satellite data for tasks such as forecasting (Shi et al., 2015), classification (Ndikumana et al., 2018) and anomaly detection (Kong et al., 2018).

In this study, we frame the damage detection problem as one of detecting anomalies in sequential InSAR coherence time series. We train an RNN on a time series of sequential InSAR coherence data taken before a damage event, then use the trained RNN to make a probabilistic forecast for the co-event InSAR coherence (i.e., the coherence of the radar echo between pre- and post-event acquisitions). The probabilistic nature of the forecast allows us to capture the distribution of the coherence values we expect for each location in the absence of any damage. We then calculate the number of standard deviations of the forecast distribution between the forecast mean and the observed co-event coherence value for each point in the region of study. The number of standard deviations between the forecast mean and observed values is used to quantify how anomalous each coherence value is, with anomalously low coherence values attributed to damage. The use of a probabilistic forecast for each pixel allows us to create a location-dependent threshold for damage which depends on the specific time series characteristics of that location.

In what follows, we summarize the underlying SAR methodology and give a brief overview of previous work on using SAR for damage mapping (Section 3.2). We then discuss how damage mapping can be formulated in terms of a machine learning problem, and present our method for deploying recurrent neural networks for damage detection (Section 3.3). We apply our method to three earthquakes, which had either substantial building damage or surface rupture (Section 3.4):

- The August 24, 2016 M_w 6.2 central Italy earthquake

- The November 12, 2017 M_w 7.3 Iran-Iraq earthquake

- The July 2019 M_w 6.4 and M_w 7.1 Ridgecrest, California, USA earthquakes.

Through these examples, we illustrate how combining a long pre-event SAR time series with RNN-based anomaly detection can improve results compared to an existing SAR damage mapping method (Section 3.5). We discuss the strengths and limitations of our proposed method (Section 3.6) then present conclusions and outline potential further work (Section 3.7). Further details of our deep learning architecture as well as the satellite data, damage assessments, and example code used in this study are presented in the supplementary materials.

3.2 Background and Previous Work

3.2.1 Synthetic Aperture Radar

Synthetic Aperture Radar (SAR) is a coherent active imaging method operating at microwave wavelengths used for mapping the Earth's surface (Ulaby & Long, 2015). The method relies on satellite-based illumination of the ground with 1–30 cm wavelength microwaves, then recording the amplitude and phase of the reflected wave. In our work, we begin with processed full-resolution data known as *single look complex* (SLC) images. Each SLC pixel in the image corresponds to a region on the Earth's surface and records the amplitude and phase of the radar echo from that region. The reflected wave depends on the properties of the Earth's surface, with the echo being a combination of the coherent sum of the backscatter from all of the reflectors within an SLC pixel, or *resolution element* (e.g., Section 3.12.2 of Simons and Rosen (2015)), as well as delays accrued during propagation through the atmosphere (e.g., Section 3.12.4.2 of Simons and Rosen (2015)).

3.2.2 Change Detection using Synthetic Aperture Radar

Changes in the imaging or viewing geometry, surface roughness, and dielectric properties of the ground within a resolution element will affect the measured radar return (Jordan et al., 2020; Zebker & Villasenor, 1992). For example, the collapse of buildings changes the path length travelled by the radar wave and randomly rearranges the radar reflectors within a given SLC pixel, leading to a random change in each SLC pixel's phase.

Comparing SAR images of the same point on Earth from the same satellite taken at different times provides proxies for changes in the Earth's surface. These measurements can be classified as coherent or incoherent, depending on whether or not the SAR phase is used (Jung & Yun, 2020). In this study, we focus on coherent change detection where the change between two SAR acquisitions can be quantified by calculating the magnitude of the complex correlation coefficient, also known as the *interferometric coherence*, or simply *coherence*, between the two complex SAR signals. For a given SLC pixel, coherence is defined as:

$$\gamma_{i,j} = \left\| \frac{|\langle \Gamma_i \Gamma_j^* \rangle|}{\sqrt{\langle |\Gamma_i|^2 \rangle \langle |\Gamma_j|^2 \rangle}} \right\|, \tag{3.1}$$

where Γ_i is the complex amplitude and phase for SAR acquisition at time step i, * represents complex conjugation, and $\langle \rangle$ denotes an ensemble average, generally approximated as a local spatial average (e.g., see Section 3.12.2.5 of Simons and Rosen (2015)). $\gamma_{i,j}$ is known as the coherence of the signal between SAR acquisitions at time steps i and j. This measure incorporates information about changes in both the amplitude and phase of the SAR signal. The coherent nature of SAR means that it is possible to sense changes on the scale of the radar wavelength (1-30 cm) when using phase information, allowing for very sensitive change detection compared to most optical data.

The use of a local spatial average in the coherence calculation means that the resolution of the coherence image is necessarily lower than the original SAR SLC image, as multiple pixels in the SLC image (SLC pixels) are used to calculate a single pixel in the coherence image (coherence pixel). Unless stated otherwise, the term *pixel* refers to coherence pixels for the rest of this paper.

For completely coherent echos $\gamma_{i,j} = 1$, whereas $\gamma_{i,j} = 0$ implies that the two echos are completely uncorrelated (a low or zero coherence value is also known as decorrelation). Stable, concrete structures, for example, will reflect radiation in the same manner through time, and thus exhibit high coherence, whereas bodies of water, which change their radar scattering properties on a time-scale of less than a second, will completely decorrelate (Bamler & Hartl, 1998).

Coherence for a given pixel will tend to decrease with the time between SAR acquisitions due to natural changes in the Earth's surface properties, with the rate of decrease depending on the rate of change of the Earth's backscattering properties at length scales similar to the radar wavelength (Zebker & Villasenor, 1992). However, the presence of seasonal effects such as snow can also lead to seasonal coherence variations as the ground surface is covered and uncovered, and rainfall can lead to sudden drops in coherence (Jordan et al., 2020). The time between the two acquisitions, known as the temporal baseline, is therefore an important indicator of how much coherence loss to expect. Increasing the spatial separation, known as the spatial baseline, between the SAR sensor's image acquisition position for repeat images will also lead to a decrease in coherence (Zebker & Villasenor, 1992). Currently orbiting satellites have tight orbital control, such that spatial baseline decorrelation is a less significant problem than it was for previous generations of sensors.

A spatial image of coherences calculated from two SAR acquisitions, acquired at different times, allows for mapping of changes in the Earth's surface properties, on the scale of the radar wavelength. For example, Simons et al. (2002) used the spatial pattern of low coherence to map the location of fault surface rupture due to the 1999 M_w 7.1 Hector Mine, California earthquake. However, decorrelation effects from regularly occurring natural processes often occur together with those induced by damage events (Jung et al., 2018). Within a coherence image spanning an earthquake (co-event coherence), we may detect decorrelation due to collapsed buildings as well as, for example, agricultural activity, vegetation growth and the changing position of vehicles in a car park, making the isolation of damage effects challenging.

The need to separate changes in surface properties due to damage from other changes motivates the framing of this problem as one of anomaly detection. If we are able to identify the nominal distribution of coherence (at a given temporal baseline) for each pixel before any damage has occurred, we can then identify which pixels have an anomalously low co-event coherence with respect to their pre-event distribution and use the presence of anomalous coherence as a proxy for damage. This nominal distribution may be a complicated function of underlying physical properties, and may not be stationary in time.

One way to characterize the pre-event coherence is to calculate the coherence between two SAR SLCs acquired as close as possible before the event. The co-event coherence can then be compared to the pre-event coherence and the magnitude of the relative coherence loss can be used to identify areas where the coherence has dropped anomalously. Generally, a threshold for the amount of coherence loss required for a pixel to be marked as damaged is chosen manually, by including areas where it is known that no damage occurred and setting the threshold so that these undamaged areas are correctly classified. This method is sometimes known as Coherence Change Detection (CCD) (e.g., see Bouaraba et al. (2012), Fielding et al. (2005), Geudtner et al. (1996), and Yun et al. (2015) and Fig. 3.1), and is based on the assumption that the calculated pre-event coherence image is a good representation of the normal pre-event coherence. In cases where coherence between sequential SAR acquisitions has a high variance (i.e., there is a lot of variation in the amount of surface change for a given temporal baseline), a single pre-event coherence image will not be a good characterization of the pre-event coherence distribution for the given temporal baseline, and the CCD damage map is likely to be noisy.

To better characterize the pre-event coherence, researchers have begun using the long time series of regular SAR acquisitions that are increasingly available (Jung et al., 2018; Karimzadeh et al., 2018). By calculating the coherence between sequential SAR acquisitions, the mean and standard deviation of the sequential pre-event coherence can be calculated for each pixel. The number of standard deviations between the mean pre-event coherence and the co-event coherence can then be used to detect anomalous co-event decreases in coherence (Olen & Bookhagen, 2018; Washaya et al., 2018). These methods rely on characterising the pre-event coherence with a single distribution through time for each pixel, which can cause problems when the coherence distribution varies substantially through time, for example due to changing precipitation with the seasons.

Additional information can be gained by calculating the coherence between all possible SAR pairs, leading to coherence images with a wide range of temporal baselines (Jordan et al., 2020; Monti-Guarnieri et al., 2018). These coherence values can be used to estimate the parameters, for each pixel, of a model for the various contributors to temporal decorrelation (Jung et al., 2016; Jung et al., 2018). This model can then be used to detect anomalies in coherence images which span the event. Similar to the mean and standard deviation method, these methods generally rely on inferring a single set of physical parameters for each pixel, without taking into account the possible variation of these parameters through time.

Supervised machine learning has also been used for damage mapping with SAR data, using comprehensive damage assessments, often available several months after major events, as ground truth to train damage classifiers (Endo et al., 2018; Y. Li et al., 2019; Wieland et al., 2016). While supervised machine learning approaches avoid the problem of manually selecting a uniform damage threshold in CCD, they

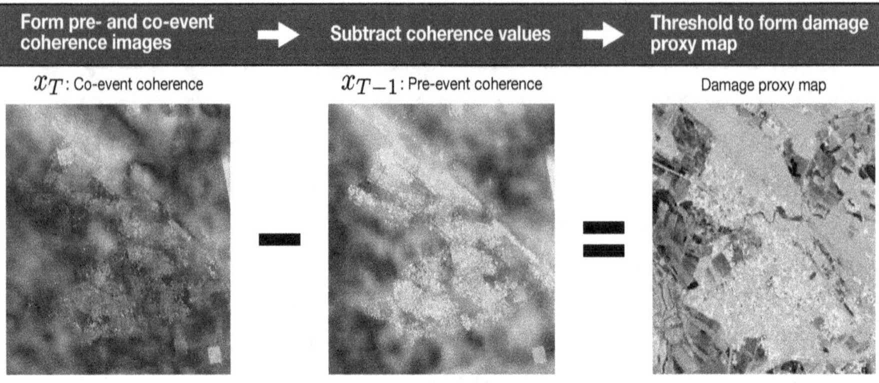

Figure 3.1:   Schematic of the existing Coherence Change Detection (CCD) method for damage mapping (Yun et al., 2015), presented for the town of Sarpol-e-Zahab, damaged during the November 2017 Iran-Iraq earthquake. A pre-event coherence image (x_{T-1}) is subtracted from the co-event coherence image (x_T) in order to calculate the coherence loss. The coherence loss is thresholded and plotted to produce a damage proxy map. Optical data from Google, CNES/Airbus, taken July 27th 2020.

rely on extensive ground truth damage assessment data for training. Additionally, if the damage classifiers are to be useful for future events, the trained classifiers must be applied to new areas and it is unclear to what extent this training readily transfers to totally different regions of the Earth's surface.

In our work, we seek to make use of all available SAR data before an event in order to make a deep learning-based, time-dependent forecast of a co-event coherence distribution that we would expect without any damage event. This approach allows us to detect anomalous changes in coherence. As we only use ground truth damage data to quantify our damage detection algorithm, and not for training, our method does not depend on ground truth damage data.

3.3 Proposed Approach

3.3.1 Notation

We have a total of $T + 2$ SAR acquisitions, ordered in time and indexed from 0 to $T + 1$; the last acquisition, $T + 1$, is post-event, while all others are pre-event. Between all pairs of consecutive acquisitions we compute the coherence values which we map to an unbounded space using a logit transform on the squared coherence (discussed below, see Eq. 3.9). We write the coherence between time steps $t - 1$ and t as $\gamma_{t,t-1}$ and the transformed coherence as x_t. Throughout the rest

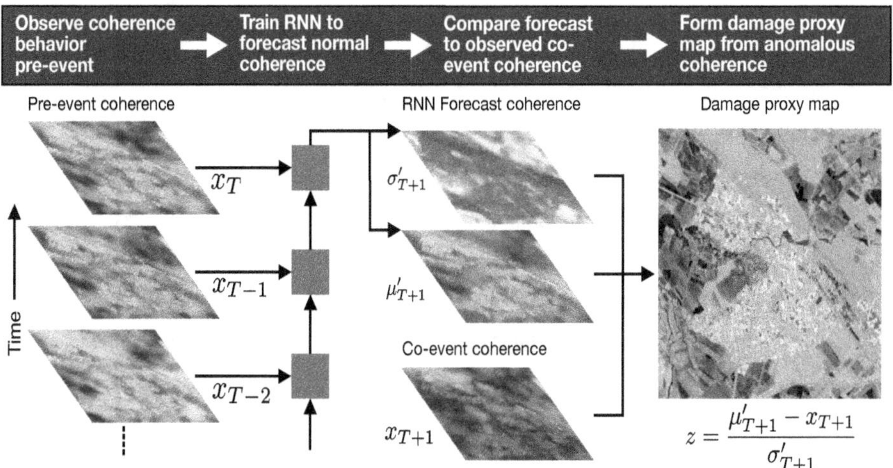

Figure 3.2: Schematic of our proposed recurrent neural network (RNN) method presented for the town of Sarpol-e-Zahab, damaged during the November 2017 Iran-Iraq earthquake. The transformed coherence values (x) are used to train a recurrent neural network to make a Gaussian forecast of the co-event coherence with mean μ'_{T+1} and standard deviation σ'_{T+1}. The forecast is compared with the observed co-event coherence, x_{T+1}, to calculate the z-score, z (see Eq. 3.10). The z-score is thresholded and plotted to produce a damage proxy map. A more detailed illustration of the neural network architecture can be found in Fig. B.1. Optical data from Google, CNES/Airbus, taken July 27th 2020.

of the paper, *coherence* refers to the transformed coherence unless otherwise stated. Let $x_{\leq T} = \{x_1, ..., x_T\}$ denote the sequence of T pre-event sequential coherence values for a given coherence pixel location, with x_{T+1} the co-event coherence. Additionally, let $\mathcal{D}_t$ denote the collection of M coherence sequences that we have available for training (i.e., coherence sequences from M different coherence pixels), each containing T pre-event coherence values. We also have $\mathcal{D}_f$, the set of coherence sequences on which we wish to perform forecasting and anomaly detection for x_{T+1}, which contains T pre-event ($x_{\leq T}$) and one co-event (x_{T+1}) coherence values for each pixel.

Our goal is to train a model that can capture the range of possible behaviors across time for the sequences in $\mathcal{D}_t$. We can then use the model to make a forecast, x'_{T+1} (we use ' to denote a forecast value), for each co-event coherence pixel in $\mathcal{D}_f$, based on the coherence time series of that pixel. We can detect anomalies by comparing the forecast with the ground truth co-event coherence value, x_{T+1}, at each pixel, mapping anomalous changes in ground surface properties that have occurred between SAR acquisitions T and $T+1$. Note that the model does not see x_{T+1}, or any damage data, during training.

3.3.2 Recurrent Neural Networks

Motivated by the sequential nature of our data, we use a recurrent neural network (RNN) as our model for forecasting the coherence time series. RNNs are a class of models frequently used on sequential data for machine learning tasks such as speech recognition, machine translation, motion tracking and time series classification and forecasting (Lipton et al., 2015; Olah, 2015). RNNs maintain a fixed-length hidden state vector, h_t, that summarizes a sequence up to time t, and is updated at every time step with observations:

$$h_t = f_\phi(h_{t-1}, x_t), \tag{3.2}$$

where f is a deterministic function, learned during training and parameterized by ϕ, and x_t is the transformed coherence (Eq. 3.9), calculated from SAR data, at time step t for a given pixel. Forecasting future values involves another function g parameterized by ψ:

$$x'_{t+1} = g_\psi(h_t). \tag{3.3}$$

In general one can optimize for parameters ϕ and ψ to minimize some loss, or cost function, between the model forecast and the coherence ground truth (here the transformed coherence values, see Eq. 3.9), for example the mean-squared error:

$$\phi^*, \psi^* = \arg\min_{\phi,\psi} \sum_{x_{\leq T} \in \mathcal{D}_t} \sum_{t=1}^{T} (x_t - x'_t)^2. \tag{3.4}$$

RNNs use neural networks as function approximators for f and g, and this optimization can be solved with some form of gradient descent (e.g., Kingma and Ba (2014)). See Section B.2 for more details.

3.3.3 Probabilistic Formulation

We aim to forecast the probability distribution over all possible values given the pre-event coherence values. This probabilistic forecast lets us evaluate the probabilities that our model assigns to the coherence values that are actually observed. We locate anomalies by identifying coherence values that have a low probability of occurring given the previous observations. To make a probabilistic forecast, we modify g in Eq. 3.3 to output the parameters of a probability distribution instead of a single value. In this work we use a Gaussian output probability, so we have:

$$[\mu'_{t+1}, \sigma'_{t+1}] = g_\psi(h_t),$$

(3.5)

where μ'_{t+1} and σ'_{t+1} are the forecast mean and standard deviation, respectively. The probability our model assigns to the ground truth co-event coherence, x_{t+1}, is then:

$$p(x_{t+1}; \mu'_{t+1}, \sigma'_{t+1}) = (2\pi\sigma'^2_{t+1})^{-\frac{1}{2}}$$
$$\times \exp\left(-\frac{\left(x_{t+1} - \mu'_{t+1}\right)^2}{2\sigma'^2_{t+1}}\right).$$

(3.6)

Instead of minimizing the mean-squared error, as shown in Eq. 3.4, the probabilistic forecast allows us to maximise the probability that our model assigns to ground truth sequences in $\mathcal{D}_t$. Computationally, probability maximization is best achieved by minimizing the negative log-likelihood that the model assigns to ground truth sequences in $\mathcal{D}_t$:

$$\phi^*, \psi^* = \arg\min_{\phi,\psi} \sum_{x_{\leq T} \in \mathcal{D}_t} -\log_e p(x_{\leq T})$$
$$= \arg\min_{\phi,\psi} \sum_{x_{\leq T} \in \mathcal{D}_t} \sum_{t=1}^{T} -\log_e p(x_t|x_{<t}),$$

(3.7)

where in the second step we factorize the conditional probabilities using the relationship $p(x_{\leq T}) = \Pi_{t=1}^{T} p(x_t|x_{<t})$. In our case, all of the information from previous elements in the time series is summarised by the μ' and σ' terms given by the forecast in Eq. 3.5, so we have that $p(x_t|x_{<t}) = p(x_t; \mu'_t, \sigma'_t)$. Therefore, combining Eq. 3.6 and Eq. 3.7 we have:

$$\phi^*, \psi^* = \arg\min_{\phi,\psi}$$
$$\sum_{x_{\leq T} \in \mathcal{D}_t} \sum_{t=1}^{T} \left(\frac{1}{2}\log_e(2\pi\sigma'^2_t) + \frac{(x_t - \mu'_t)^2}{2\sigma'^2_t}\right).$$

(3.8)

Eq. 3.8 gives us a loss function that takes into account both the mean and standard deviation of the forecast, allowing us to optimize a probabilistic forecast for the coherence. We can optimize for the parameters in Eq. 3.8 using some form of gradient descent (e.g., Kingma and Ba (2014)).

Note that a Gaussian distribution assigns nonzero probability everywhere in $\mathbb{R}$, a distribution that is inconsistent with coherence as defined in Eq. 3.1, which is by definition bounded (i.e., $\gamma_{t-1,t} \in [0, 1]$). We therefore transform the coherence to an unbounded space before training the RNN. We choose the inverse-sigmoid transform (also known as the logit transform) on the square of the coherence values:

$$x_t = S^{-1}(\gamma_{t-1,t}^2) = \log_e \left(\frac{\gamma_{t-1,t}^2}{1 - \gamma_{t-1,t}^2} \right), \tag{3.9}$$

which maps the domain from $[0, 1]$ to $(-\infty, \infty)$. This choice of transform is motivated by near mathematical equivalence between the logit transform of coherence squared and the logarithm of the variance of the interferometric phase, see Section B.1 for more details. We refer to the new unbounded space as the logit space. Our model will then forecast Gaussian distributions over the unbounded logit space.

3.3.4 Model and Training Details

The RNN model we use in this work (represented by f_ϕ in Eq. 3.2) is called a gated recurrent unit (GRU), chosen for its ability to learn long-term dependencies in time series (Cho et al., 2014). The hidden state output from f_ϕ is fed into a feed-forward neural network, represented by g_ψ (Eq. 3.5) which then outputs the parameters of the forecast distribution. To find the optimum model parameters (Eq. 3.8), we train the model using the Adam optimizer (Kingma & Ba, 2014). See Section B.2 for more details of the model and training, as well as further references. An implementation of our deep learning model can be found on GitHub: https://github.com/olliestephenson/dpm-rnn-public.

3.3.5 Anomaly Detection for Co-event Coherence

To construct a proxy for damage we normalize the difference between the forecast co-event mean, μ'_{T+1}, and the observed co-event coherence, x_{T+1}, by the standard deviation of the forecast σ'_{T+1}. This quantity is termed the z-score, which we define as:

$$z = \frac{\mu'_{T+1} - x_{T+1}}{\sigma'_{T+1}}. \tag{3.10}$$

Note that we have switched the order of μ'_{T+1} and x_{T+1} terms compared to usual definition of the z-score. With this definition, a large positive z-score implies that the coherence is many standard deviations below the forecast coherence, i.e., we have an anomalous drop in coherence, possibly due to damage. We use this definition of the z-score as the basis of our proxy for damage.

3.4   Data

3.4.1   Coherence Calculation

We use data from the Copernicus Sentinel-1 satellites, a pair of C-band SAR satellites operated by the European Space Agency. We download freely available Level-1 Single Look Complex (SLC) images acquired in interferometric wideswath mode (European Space Agency, n.d.). We then create a coregistered stack of SLCs covering the region of interest. To generate coherence values, as defined in Eq. 3.1, we average over a rectangle, or chip, of SLC pixels. In this case we use a chip of 15 SLC pixels in range (across the satellite track) and 5 in azimuth (along the satellite track) corresponding to a region of approximately 50 m by 70 m. Note that the resolution in range (across-track) of Sentinel-1 SLCs is higher than in the azimuth (along-track) direction. As stated above, the use of a chip to calculate coherence means that the coherence map is lower resolution than the SLC image as each coherence pixel contains information from a 50 m by 70 m area.

For each study area, we produce two separate coherence data sets: one for training the network ($\mathcal{D}_t$), and one for forecasting purposes ($\mathcal{D}_f$). We construct the training data set to have a large number of pixels drawn from a wide area surrounding the area of interest, while the forecasting data set focuses just on the area of interest to be mapped. More details on how these data sets are constructed can be found in Section B.3.

3.4.2   Study Areas

In this study, we consider three earthquakes:

August 24, 2016 M_w 6.2 central Italy earthquake

This event destroyed much of the town of Amatrice in central Italy. (United States Geological Survey, 2016). The Copernicus Emergency Management Service produced a damage map assessing the damage level of every building in the town (Copernicus Emergency Management Service, 2016). This comprehensive damage assessment allows us to quantitatively validate the RNN and CCD methods against the known damage levels.

November 12, 2017 M_w 7.3 Iran-Iraq earthquake

This event damaged the city of Sarpol-e-Zahab on the Iran-Iraq border (United States Geological Survey, 2017). The United Nations Institute for Training and

Research (UNITAR) produced a damage map for Sarpol-e-Zahab in the wake of the earthquake (United Nations Institute for Training and Research, 2017), allowing for a qualitative test of our damage proxy map and comparison with the CCD method.

July 2019 M_w 6.4 and M_w 7.1 Ridgecrest, California, USA earthquakes

To explore the ability of our method to capture other forms of anomalous ground disturbances, we also consider the Ridgecrest earthquakes which struck the Mojave desert, California, in early July 2019. The Ridgecrest sequence contained two earthquakes with substantial surface rupture tens of kilometers long: an M_w 6.4 event on July 4th, and, 34 hours later, an M_w 7.1 event (Kendrick et al., 2019; Ponti et al., 2020; Ross, Idini, et al., 2019). The earthquakes also caused liquefaction, small rock falls and minor damage to buildings (Brandenberg et al., 2019; Hough et al., 2020; Zimmaro et al., 2020). The mapping of surface ruptures and location of liquefaction allows us to qualitatively compare the damage map to the location of known ground surface changes.

In Section B.3, we give more detailed information about these three earthquakes and the available data for each event.

3.5   Results

We present damage proxy maps for the coherence change detection (CCD) and our proposed RNN methods, then use available independent damage data to validate the efficacy of each method. For each method, we calculate a numerical damage proxy for every pixel, then threshold that damage proxy to create damage proxy maps. For Sarpol-e-Zahab and Ridgecrest, the limited nature of the ground truth data only allows for a qualitative comparison between the methods. For Amatrice, however, more comprehensive ground truth allows us to carry out a quantitative comparison. For Sarpol-e-Zahab, we also explore the forecasts the RNN makes through time for pixels in different locations. We find that the RNN method yields qualitative and quantitative improvements over the the CCD method.

August 24, 2016 M_w 6.2 earthquake, Amatrice, Italy

Fig. 3.3 shows the RNN method applied to mapping the damage in the town of Amatrice due to the August 24, 2016 central Italy earthquake. We use ground truth damage data from the Copernicus Emergency Management Service (Copernicus Emergency Management Service, 2016) to choose an optimum threshold for damage (discussed below), and mask values below that threshold. Details of the damage

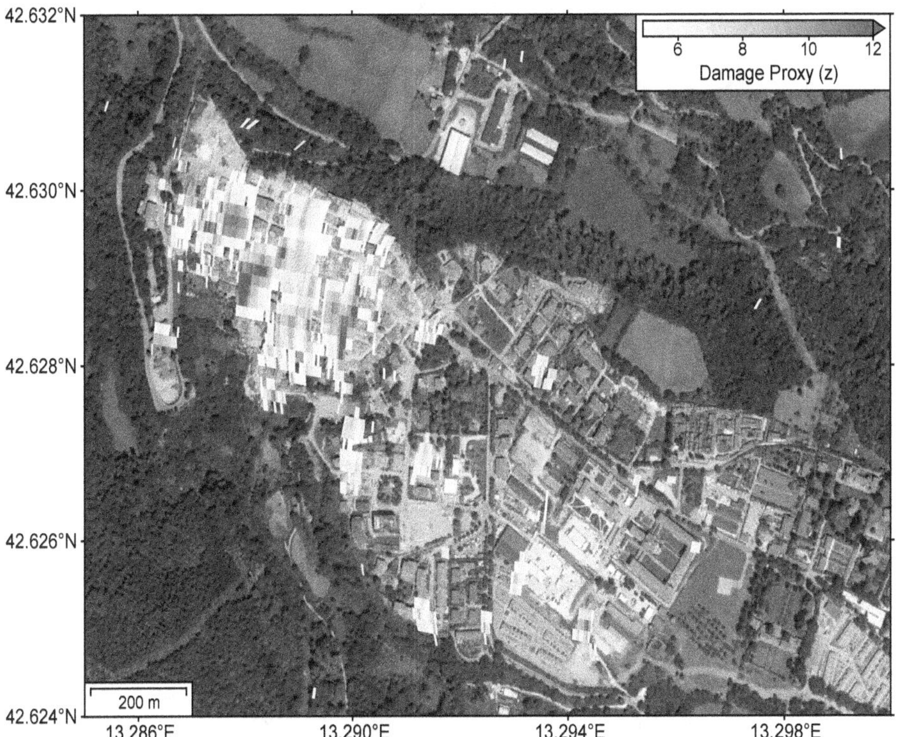

Figure 3.3: RNN DPM for the town of Amatrice, Italy, badly damaged during the 2016 M_w 6.2 central Italy earthquake. The center of the town, which was largely destroyed, is clearly highlighted by elevated damage proxy values towards the top left of the map. Z-score values below 4.93 (chosen from the $F_{0.5}$ score, Eq. 3.11) are masked, values above 12 are set to red as indicated by the color bar. Ground truth damage data are presented in Figure B.3. Optical imagery from Google, taken July 6th 2017.

data are presented in Section B.3. The ground truth damage data also allows for a direct quantitative comparison between the CCD and RNN methods.

We seek to classify each coherence chip as either "damaged" or "undamaged" and compare the classification ability of the CCD and RNN methods. Comparing the classifiers relies on assigning each chip a score (the z-score for the RNN method and the coherence loss for the CCD method), setting a threshold for damage, and then comparing the damaged/undamaged classifications with the ground truth. For every set of classifications, we have four categories: assigned damaged and truly damaged (true positive), assigned damaged but actually undamaged (false positive),

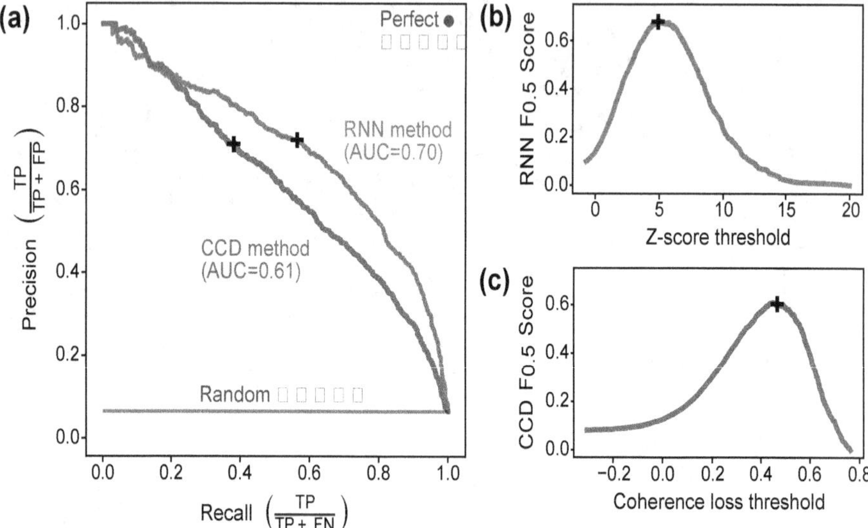

Figure 3.4: Quality metrics for the CCD and RNN damage classification methods. (a) Precision-recall curves for Amatrice damage proxy maps using the CCD (blue line) and RNN (red line) methods. For a perfect classifier we can choose a threshold that gives precision and recall equal to one, indicated in the top right corner. A random classifier gives a constant precision, equal to the fraction of the data set that is truly damaged, with recall varying with the threshold, indicated by the grey horizontal line at the bottom of the plot. The larger area under the curve (AUC) for the RNN method indicates improved performance. The black crosses show the position of maximum $F_{0.5}$ score identified in figures (b) and (c). (b) $F_{0.5}$ score (see Eq. 3.11) for varying z-score damage thresholds using the RNN method. (c) $F_{0.5}$ score for varying coherence loss damage thresholds using the CCD method.

assigned undamaged and truly undamaged (true negative) and assigned undamaged but actually damaged (false negative).

In this case the ground truth damage data are building footprints, each with a damage score, which we separate into "damaged" and "undamaged" classes (see Section B.3). To determine the ground truth associated with each coherence chip, we calculate the proportion of each chip's area that is occupied by damaged buildings. Coherence chips that have at least one third of their area (roughly 1200 m^2, see the discussion in Section 3.6) occupied by the footprints of damaged buildings, we assign to be truly damaged. Note that as the radar is side-looking, the 3D nature of the buildings means their radar footprint does not exactly match their ground footprint, a fact that we do not take into account in this work.

To compare the two methods quantitatively, we use a standard precision-recall curve (Davis & Goadrich, 2006) (Fig. 3.4). We calculate precision (the fraction of chips classified as damaged that are actually damaged) and recall (the fraction of truly damaged chips that are classified as damaged) for a range of damage proxy thresholds for each method. For a general classifier that is imperfect but better than random, precision and recall will trade off against one another. For example, with a high threshold, only a few points will be classified as damaged, and many of these will be truly damaged, leading to a high precision. However, with a high threshold the recall is low as most truly damaged points are incorrectly classified as undamaged. A low threshold means that many of the damaged points are above the threshold; however, there are also many false positives, leading to low precision and high recall. As our classes are unbalanced (there are many more undamaged points than damaged points) the precision-recall curve is preferred over the receiver operating characteristic (ROC) curve that is also used to assess the quality of classifiers (Davis & Goadrich, 2006).

Different classification methods can be quantitatively compared by calculating the area under the precision-recall curve (known as PR AUC). A perfect classifier will have an area of unity, with better algorithms having PR AUCs closer to this value. The PR AUC for a random classifier will be equal to the fraction of the data set that is truly damaged. Note that the PR AUC is distinct from the ROC AUC which is also used to compare classifiers (Berrar & Flach, 2012). Our PR AUC results presented in Fig. 3.4(a) show a clear quantitative improvement when using the RNN method over the CCD method, with a PR AUC of 0.70 for the RNN method and 0.61 for the CCD method. We achieve this improvement using the RNN method in spite of the relatively poor quality training data (see discussion in Section 3.6).

To compute the optimum threshold for damage for each method, we can use the F_β score, which is the weighted harmonic mean of the precision and the recall, computed as:

$$F_\beta = (1 + \beta^2) \frac{\text{precision} \cdot \text{recall}}{(\beta^2 \cdot \text{precision}) + \text{recall}}. \tag{3.11}$$

F_β will vary with the threshold, and we can choose a threshold that maximizes the score. This weighting considers recall β times as important as precision. In our case we set $\beta = 0.5$ and thus compute the $F_{0.5}$ score for all possible thresholds for both methods. Our choice of β weights precision as twice as important as recall, based on the assumption that we wish to direct finite emergency response resources to the places most likely to be damaged and thus favor higher precision at the expense

Table 3.1: Optimum threshold and corresponding precision and recall values for both methods using the Amatrice data set, selected using the maximum value of the $F_{0.5}$ score, along with the area under the precision-recall curves (PR AUC).

Method	Optimum threshold	Optimum precision	Optimum recall	PR AUC
RNN	4.93	0.72	0.56	0.70
CCD	0.47	0.71	0.38	0.61

of lower recall. At the maximum $F_{0.5}$ values, both methods have a precision just over 0.7, meaning over 70% of the points classified as damaged are truly damaged; however, the RNN method has recall of 0.56, compared to 0.38 for the CCD method, a clear quantitative improvement. The $F_{0.5}$ scores are presented in Fig. 3.4(**b**) and (**c**), and the optimum threshold and corresponding precision and recall for each method are given in Table 3.1.

Note that we perform the quantification on a pixel-by-pixel basis (using coherence pixels) rather than a building-by-building basis. Building areas can vary greatly, and, for the same level of damage, a small building and a large building can have very different effects on the coherence. Therefore a building-by-building quantification would combine metrics with very different sensitivities, whereas in theory each coherence chip should respond in a more similar way when a given fraction of its area is occupied by buildings with the same level of damage. We also note that in actual deployment scenarios, building footprints may not be available, and we may also be interested in investigating other forms of anomalous surface change (for example fault ruptures and landslides).

November 12, 2017 M_w 7.3 earthquake, Sarpol-e-Zahab, Iran-Iraq Border

In Fig. 3.5, we present damage proxy maps for the town of Sarpol-e-Zahab, damaged during the Iran-Iraq earthquake of November 12, 2017, for both the CCD and RNN methods. Using results from Amatrice (Table 3.1) the threshold for damage is set at $z = 4.93$ for the RNN method, and coherence loss = 0.47 for the CCD method, with damage proxies below these thresholds masked out. For display purposes we again choose the upper limit of the RNN color bar to be $z = 12$ and set the limit of the CCD color bar such that the same number of points are above the color bar limit as for the RNN case to provide a fair visual comparison. The damage data from the UN (United Nations Institute for Training and Research, 2017) (Figure B.4) allows us to qualitatively compare the damage maps to the documented damage in the city.

Within the city, both methods highlight neighborhoods where the UN located many collapsed buildings (for example in the northwest of the city) However, they also have elevated damage proxies over areas in the city where the UN did not record damage, possibly due to the sensitivity of InSAR coherence to small changes in surface properties, and possibly due to significant damage that was missed in the UN damage map. This seems to be more significant for the RNN method, which finds a larger amount of damage in the city than the CCD method.

Looking outside the city yields a clearer difference between the methods. In Fig. 3.5, we use white dashed lines to highlight several areas where the CCD method has agricultural fields outside the city with high damage scores that are no longer highlighted in the RNN damage map, indicating that the co-event coherence for these areas was within the bounds of the normal variability for those pixels. This difference between the methods indicates the advantage of taking into account the full temporal behavior of each pixel. In Fig. 3.5, we also highlight one area outside the city where the RNN method has a higher damage proxy than the CCD method. As this area is over a rocky ridge, it is possible that the RNN damage proxy is capturing surface change due to rockfalls caused by the earthquake shaking.

To better understand the damage map produced by the RNN, we select four locations in and around the town that show different styles of coherence time series. We apply this analysis to Sarpol-e-Zahab due to the larger amount of pre-event data compared to Amatrice, and the wider variety of pixel behaviors in a small area compared to Ridgecrest. In Fig. 3.6, we present the coherence time series, as well as the mean and standard deviation of the RNN coherence forecast and resulting z-score through time. For each case, the forecast at each time step is made based on Eq. 3.5, using the hidden state that is output from the trained model with the input being the coherence time series at that pixel up to that time.

For pixel (**a**) of Fig. 3.6, over a rocky ridge, we see a high, stable coherence through time, with no substantial drop in coherence co-seismically, hence a low co-event z-score. Pixel (**b**) is over a river, where surface properties change rapidly between SAR acquisitions, hence the pixel has a low coherence and higher uncertainty, but again has no co-event drop in coherence. Pixel (**c**) is within one of the badly damaged areas of the town. The pre-event coherence is high and relatively stable through time, causing a narrow uncertainty in the forecast. The co-event coherence is around 19 standard deviations below the forecast ($z \approx 19$), implying that the pixel is well out of the bounds of normal behavior. We infer that this is due to building damage. Finally,

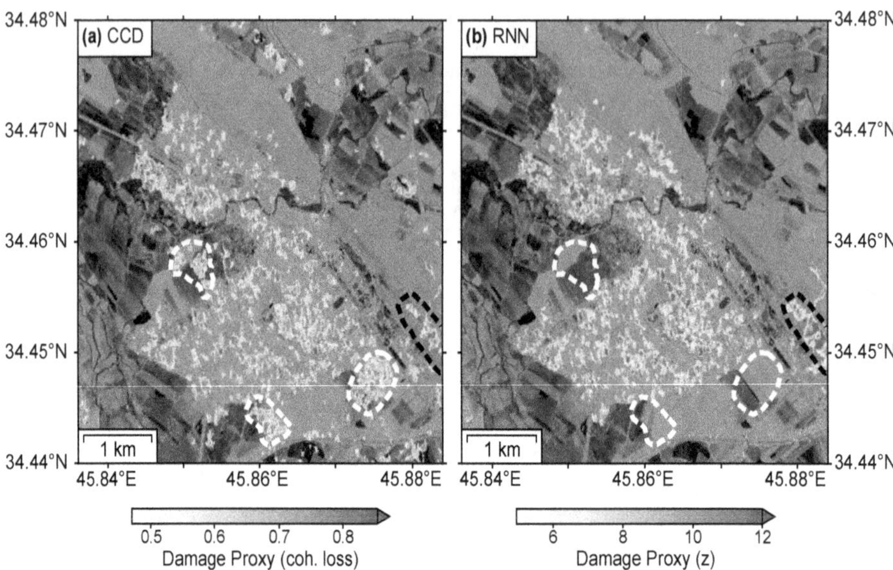

Figure 3.5: Comparison of CCD **(a)** and RNN **(b)** DPMs for Sarpol-e-Zahab, damaged in the November 12, 2017 M_w 7.3 Iran-Iraq earthquake. For each plot we mask values below a threshold, with the threshold chosen using the maximum value of the $F_{0.5}$ curve for the Amatrice data set (see Table 3.1). The upper threshold of the color scales are chosen such that both plots have the same number of points above the threshold. The white dashed lines highlight example areas where the CCD method gives false positive damage detection in regions outside of the city that are no longer classified as damaged by the proposed RNN method. The black dashed line shows an area over a rocky ridge where greater damage is shown by the RNN method compared to the CCD method. Ground truth damage data are presented in Figure B.4. Optical imagery from Google, CNES/Airbus, taken July 27th 2020.

pixel **(d)**, covering an agricultural field, has highly variable coherence through time, which causes a large variance in the forecast coherence. The co-event coherence is substantially below the final pre-event coherence, meaning the CCD method shows elevated damage proxy values. However, in the context of the entire time series we see that this coherence is well within the bounds of the forecast coherence variability and thus the z-score is small.

July 2019 Ridgecrest earthquakes, California, USA

The earthquakes that struck near the town of Ridgecrest, California, in July 2019 (Ross, Idini, et al., 2019) provide an opportunity to test our proposed method on other forms of anomalous changes in ground surface properties, including fault

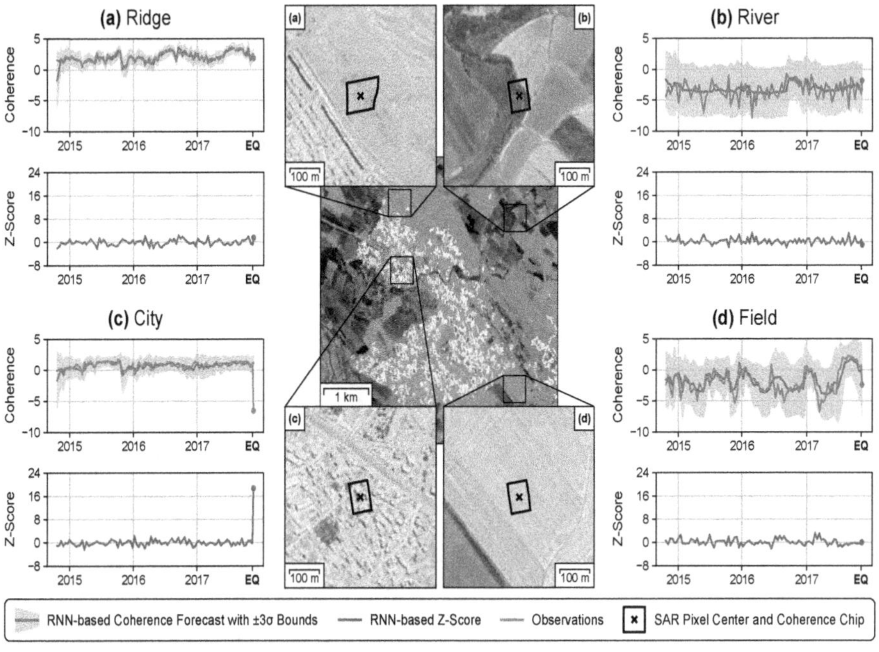

Figure 3.6: Sarpol-e-Zahab RNN damage map along with coherence time series and Gaussian forecasts for four representative locations ((**a**)-(**d**)) around the city. The z-score indicates the number of standard deviations between the forecast and the ground truth, and the coherence is plotted in logit space (i.e., it has been transformed into an unbounded space, see Eq. 3.9). Note that the shape of the coherence chip on the ground changes depending on the topography due to the way SAR data is acquired. The "Coherence" plotted on the y-axis is the logit transform of the squared coherence (Eq. 3.9). Optical imagery from Google, CNES/Airbus, taken July 27th 2020.

surface rupture, landslides and liquefaction (Brandenberg et al., 2019; Hough et al., 2020; Kendrick et al., 2019; Ponti et al., 2020; Zimmaro et al., 2020). In Fig. 3.7, we plot the RNN damage proxy map with two different z-score thresholds. The higher threshold allow us to focus on points that have had more anomalous coherence drops compared to their previous behavior through time. Using a threshold of $z = 4.93$ from the Amatrice data above (Fig. 3.7 (**a**)) we see that the largest anomalies lie on the M_w 7.1 and M_w 6.4 surface ruptures (running NW-SE and NE-SW, respectively) and liquefaction in the Searles Lakebed area, around (35.6°N, 117.3°W).

In Fig. 3.7 (**b**), we plot all points below $z = 0$ as black, more clearly showing smaller coherence anomalies surrounding the ruptures. Comparison with the mapped ruptures shows that some of these anomalies are due to smaller off fault ruptures, and we can also locate a small amount of damage in the town of Ridgecrest (Hough et al., 2020). The correlation with topographic slope of many of the smaller anomalies (for example around (35.80°N, 117.50°W)) suggest that these are due to small rockfalls or landslides induced by the earthquake. Damage maps such as these could be useful for directing mapping of ground failure in the aftermath of earthquakes.

3.6 Discussion

3.6.1 Importance of the training data

The goal of the RNN method is to produce the best possible forecast of the distribution of the co-event coherence value at each location, in the absence of any damage, given that location's pre-event coherence time series and the trained model. The forecast at every location depends on the trained model and thus contains information from every coherence time series used in the training. In this way, every forecast uses information learned from a wide spatial area.

Different parts of a given geographic region will be affected by processes that affect coherence (e.g., rain and snow) in a similar fashion, meaning that some amount of correlation between coherence time series in the region is likely. For example, a storm could cause consistent amounts of change in the surface properties across a wide area, leading to a sudden, correlated drop in coherence for many of the time series in the region.

When training the RNN, we split the overall training set $\mathcal{D}_t$ into training ($\mathcal{D}_{t,t}$) and validation ($\mathcal{D}_{t,v}$) components. $\mathcal{D}_{t,t}$ is used to optimize the RNN parameters, whereas $\mathcal{D}_{t,v}$ is used to evaluate the model performance according to Eq. 3.7 and choose the model with the best loss (note the ultimate task of damage classification is not part of model selection). When the training set $\mathcal{D}_t$ is split into its training and validation components, any correlation between time series from the same geographic area could lead to *data leakage* (Kaufman et al., 2011), whereby information from the validation set can also be found in the training set.

Data leakage can result in the RNN making artificially good forecasts as the RNN memorizes correlated patterns in the data, effectively over-fitting rather than learning generalizable rules. For example, we might get an unexpectedly good forecast of a sudden coherence drop in a time series which the RNN had not previously seen, due to the same pattern also being present in time series used in training. A possible case of this can be seen in time series (**a**) of Fig. 3.6; in late 2015 there is a sudden drop in

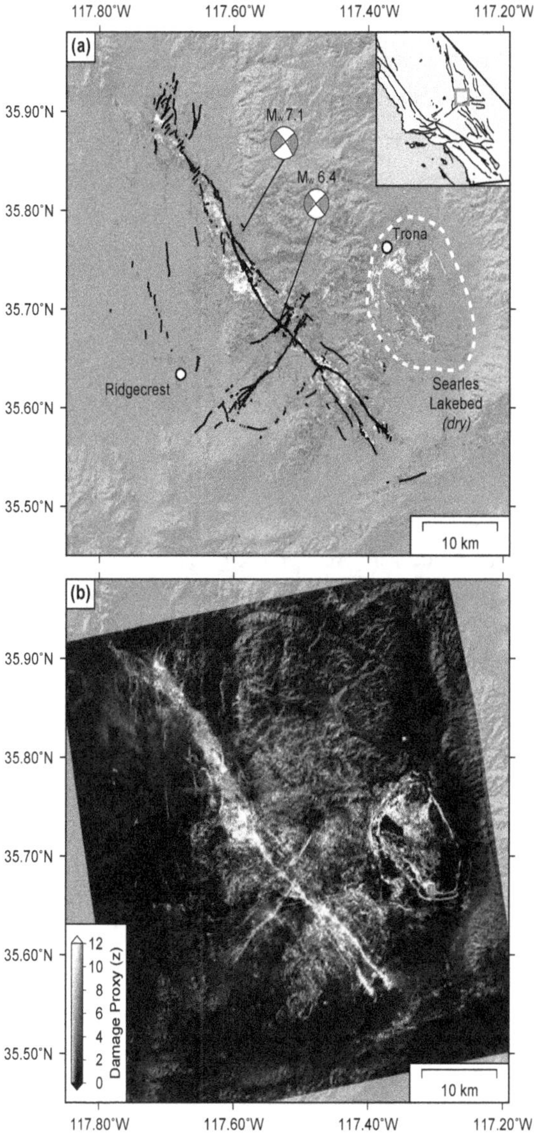

Figure 3.7: Ridgecrest RNN damage proxy map with different thresholds. **(a)** All points with $z < 4.93$ are masked. Black lines indicate mapped surface ruptures from Ponti *et al.* (Ponti et al., 2020). The white dashed line indicates the approximate extent of the dry Searles Lakebed that saw substantial liquefaction (Zimmaro et al., 2020). Global CMT focal mechanisms are plotted for the M$_w$ 6.4 and M$_w$ 7.1 earthquakes (Dziewonski et al., 1981; Ekström et al., 2012). The inset shows a regional map with simplified Quaternary faults. **(b)** Same damage proxy map as **(a)** except with no masking and points with $z < 0$ plotted in black. This threshold allows less intense off-fault anomalous change to be more clearly seen.

coherence (from around 3 to 0 in logit space) which is closely mirrored by the mean and variance of the forecast distribution. It seems unlikely that this coherence drop would be so accurately forecastable unless the network had seen many examples of similar patterns during training. Ideally, the network would instead learn that sudden drops in coherence can occur, and would broaden its uncertainty (i.e., the forecast standard deviation) accordingly.

Since data leakage can lead to artificially high performance on supervised machine learning tasks (Kaufman et al., 2011), we ask if data leakage during RNN training could lead to artificially improved damage classification. In our case, there can be no leakage of the actual ground truth damage data, which is the target for our RNN-based classifier but is not used in training. There can only be leakage in correlated patterns in the pre-event coherence time series. As detailed above, data leakage could cause over-fitting, making the forecast overly confident, i.e., with a standard deviation (σ') that is too small. An overly confident forecast will lead to a z-score that is larger for the same difference between observed coherence (x) and the mean of the forecast (μ'), making the z-score noisier and meaning the likely result of data leakage is a worse performing damage classifier, not one with artificially improved performance.

The quality of the RNN forecast will depend on the training data which we use. In general, training data acquired over a shorter time span and over a smaller spatial area will not sample the full scope of representative coherence behavior. We expect that more limited training data will cause the model to give a less representative forecast coherence distribution, as the network will see fewer examples of how coherence can vary in time and space. In Section B.4, we explore how decreasing the time span of the training data affects the quality of the damage map for the Amatrice example, finding that the results are highly variable when less than a year of data is used. Based on these results, we emphasize the importance of testing the RNN method on a wider variety of disasters, in different geographic regions, to ensure robust performance.

A smaller geographic region is more likely to have strongly correlated coherence time series, leading to more significant data leakage problems and over-fitting during training. Drawing pixels from a very wide geographic area, or potentially many different geographic areas all over the Earth, could ameliorate this problem. A systematic exploration of the relationship between the input SAR data and the quality of the final damage map is beyond the scope of this paper.

Coherence images with longer temporal baselines will generally have lower coherence than images from a similar time period and region with a shorter temporal baseline (Zebker & Villasenor, 1992). Our current RNN training approach ignores the temporal baseline of the coherence images, effectively assuming that all coherence images have the same temporal baseline. However, our coherence time series have some variation in temporal baselines due to the varying acquisition frequency of Sentinel-1 SAR data, with the repeat frequency tending to become more stable and more frequent with time (see Section B.3 for details of the data). A variable temporal baseline adds an extra noise term due to changing amounts of temporal decorrelation. Therefore, the likely effect of a variable temporal baseline is to make the coherence time series noisier, thus decreasing the confidence of the forecast and reducing the sensitivity to damage.

For the Amatrice case, the timing of the event meant that we had less than two years of Sentinel-1 data preceding the earthquake, and the data had a higher variance in the temporal baseline. The lack of data and variable temporal baseline degrades the performance of the RNN, so the precision-recall results presented are likely a lower bound on the possible performance for damage mapping in this area.

3.6.2 Sensitivity to damage in different geographic areas

Random motion of scatterers within a resolution element on the scale of the wavelength of the satellite radar signal ($\approx$5.6 cm for this work) will cause decorrelation between two radar echoes (Zebker & Villasenor, 1992). Different regions of any study area will have different background rates of change in their surface properties, and these rates may vary through time. High rates of surface change will lead to low coherence, and variability through time in the rate of change will create a larger standard deviation in the coherence time series.

Robust damage detection relies on separating normal changes from damage induced changes, and the ability to do this separation depends on the rate of surface change and how much this rate varies in time. At a given time step, for a given pixel, the RNN forecasts the average rate of change with the mean of the forecast (μ'), and the variability with its standard deviation (σ'), both of which are used to calculate the z-score (Eq. 3.10). A high background rate of surface change will lead to a low μ', thus obscuring coherence drops due to damage as $\mu' - x$ will be small. Similarly, large coherence variability will cause larger σ' values leading to smaller z-scores, making it hard to separate coherence drops that are natural from those that are damage induced.

Differing behavior of pixels means that, for two different pixels, the same z-score does not necessarily imply the same level of damage, but instead the same ratio of coherence change to background coherence variability. Thus, when interpreting the z-score map, it may also be useful to consider the forecast mean and standard deviation to understand the noise level for each pixel, with low mean and high standard deviation indicating noisy pixels and thus lower sensitivity to damage. We note that stable, human-made structures typically have higher and less variable coherence, whereas areas with vegetation, water and snow typically have lower and more variable coherence.

For the Ridgecrest damage proxy map (Fig. 3.7), it is noticeable that the largest z-scores appear to correspond to the most significant ground disruption, specifically the surface ruptures from the M_w 6.4 and M_w 7.1 earthquakes and liquefaction near the town of Trona (Brandenberg et al., 2019; Hough et al., 2020; Zimmaro et al., 2020). The apparent link between z-score magnitude and intensity of ground surface change may be due to the desertic conditions in the area. The dry, stable conditions mean that most pixels have similar behavior through time, i.e., they have a similar noise level, meaning z-scores are more directly comparable between pixels. More generally, we should be able to use z-scores as proxies for levels of damage within groups of pixels that have similar forecast standard deviations. However, the z-score is less comparable between groups of pixels with very different forecast means and standard deviations.

The desertic conditions in the Ridgecrest area mean that coherence is comparatively high and stable through time. Because of this stability, the single pre-event image used in the CCD method is a better proxy for the pre-event coherence than the single images used in the other regions, causing the RNN and CCD methods to be more similar than for the other two case studies (we do not present the CCD results here).

Damaged buildings that are smaller or on poorly orientated slopes with respect to the satellite line of sight will occupy a smaller fraction of the coherence chip. These buildings will therefore have a smaller effect on the coherence, making them harder to identify using coherence based methods. The choice of the fraction of the chip area which has to be occupied by damaged buildings in order for that chip to be in the "truly damaged" class can therefore have a substantial effect on the final precision-recall area under the curve (PR AUC) values for the Amatrice data set.

We choose one third of the chip area (roughly 1200 m^2) as it gives approximately the largest PR AUC values, although the change in PR AUC values between fractions of 20% and 50% are small (RNN PR AUC in the range 0.68-0.70) The decrease of the RNN PR AUC below 20% building fraction suggests that our method has difficulty identifying damage where the damaged area occupies less than around 700 m^2 of the coherence chip, meaning, for example, our method could have difficulties correctly classifying an isolated damaged building that is smaller than 25 m × 25 m. With the present resolution, this method is likely most useful for detecting large damaged buildings and damaged blocks, rather than damage to individual smaller buildings.

3.6.3   The choice of change metric and forecast distribution

While coherence has proven useful for surface change detection, metrics such as the SAR amplitude correlation can also be used (Jung & Yun, 2020). Using the amplitude can be particularly useful when the InSAR coherence is low. We suspect that a similar RNN-based anomaly detection approach would also work on time series of other metrics used for SAR change detection, and could also be combined with the coherence metric; however, we do not pursue this here.

When calculating coherence, we approximate an ensemble average for a given SLC pixel with a spatial average around that SLC pixel when evaluating Eq. 3.1 (e.g., see Section 3.12.2.5 of Simons and Rosen (2015)). In our case, we use a local chip (15 by 5 SLC pixels in size) and assume that these SLC pixels are drawn from the same statistical distribution of amplitude and phase. There is a trade off in the choice of chip size—smaller chips are more likely to combine pixels that demonstrate the same statistics through time (as a result of being over the same type of land surface). However, they also contain fewer samples with which to estimate the coherence, leading to a larger variance in the estimate and a noisier coherence time series. Larger coherence chips contain more samples, but are more likely to include SLC pixels with greater differences in statistical behavior through time, less consistent with the assumption that we used to approximate the ensemble average. Larger chips also provide lower spatial resolution. Limited testing with the data presented in this study indicates that the results are made worse by reducing the chip size to 9 by 3 SLC pixels; however, we have not systematically explored how the results vary with chip size.

The choice of forecasting a Gaussian distribution on the logit transform of coherence squared is motivated by the desire to use an unbounded distribution on an unbounded space, and the mathematical relationship to the logarithm of the phase variance (Section B.1). However, the specific transform and distribution are ad-hoc and in general they may not produce the optimal forecast. We leave the exploration of the best transform and distribution to future work.

Rather than using a local chip to estimate coherence, a stack of SAR images can be used to identify a non-local neighborhood of SLC pixels, within some distance of a central SLC pixel, that behave in a statistically similar pattern through time. The coherence can then be evaluated over those SLC pixels, which has been shown to give a better coherence estimate (Ferretti et al., 2011). However, using a non-local coherence evaluation introduces problems when doing damage mapping. Damage will change the statistical characteristics of an SLC pixel, meaning that co-event SLC pixels may no longer be in their pre-event statistical groupings. For example, some of the SLC pixels may be over collapsed buildings, with other SLC pixels over buildings that remained undamaged. On the other hand, SLC pixels in a local chip are more likely to have been affected by the same process (e.g., building collapse). Thus, while a non-local coherence calculation may give improved results for pre-event coherence calculations, our method requires us to use a local chip for the coherence calculation.

3.6.4 Near real-time deployment

When deploying damage mapping for rapid response, delivering timely products, ideally within hours, is exceptionally important. While the wait time for a Sentinel-1 post-event acquisition could be up to six days, in many cases we will have an image before this, allowing the information to feed in to rapid disaster response. Other SAR satellites also acquire data; however, they do not have the same long time series of open access acquisitions that is available from Sentinel-1. Planned SAR missions, such as NISAR (Sharma, 2019) and ALOS-4 (Motohka et al., 2019) should improve the availability of frequently acquired SAR data.

A near real-time deployment could follow this workflow, which would ideally be almost completely automated:

1. Identify the natural disaster

2. Find the SAR satellite which has a sufficient time series of existing observations, and will have an overflight of the affected area in the immediate future

3. Download the existing SAR data, coregister, and calculate a coherence time series

4. Train the RNN and forecast the co-event coherence

5. Obtain the first post-event acquisition, coregister and calculate co-event coherence

6. Compare with the forecast to calculate the damage proxy map

7. Inspect DPM and distribute to first responders via previously established channels of communication, ensuring that they have a clear understanding of the information the damage proxy map is providing.

The most computationally demanding step of this process is the coregistration of the large quantities of pre-event SAR data, with the coherence time series calculation and RNN training also requiring substantial computational resources. Combined, these steps can take several days of computing using our current codes and resources, potentially impacting response times. However, steps 1–4 do not necessarily affect the post-disaster response time, as they can either be pre-computed and regularly updated, or in some cases, be completed before the essential post-event acquisition becomes available. Additionally, the use of cloud computing resources and improved algorithms can greatly decrease processing time. Free and open data, accessible with minimal latency, are vital for the effective deployment of such a disaster monitoring system.

The quality of the damage map could be further enhanced by combination with other damage assessments, e.g., maps of shaking intensity and on-the-ground reports, as well as previously identified zones of higher risk for building collapse, fault surface rupture, landslides and liquefaction (Loos et al., 2020).

3.7 Conclusions

In this work, we present a deep learning-based damage mapping algorithm for synthetic aperture radar (SAR) sequential coherence time series. Coherence represents a proxy for ground surface change, and thus by separating out anomalous from expected coherence values after a natural disaster we can find regions that have had anomalous surface change, potentially due to building collapse, surface rupture, landslides or other hazards. We use a recurrent neural network to learn the normal behavior of coherence through time by training on SAR coherence time series spanning a large area, then forecast the probability distribution of the coherence we expect without any disaster. We then use the deviation between the observed and forecast coherence to locate anomalous coherence changes, which we assume to be due to collapsed buildings. A comparison with on-the-ground building damage assessments shows that this method is quantitatively better than an alternative method of damage mapping based on coherence loss. We discuss the advantages and limitations of our proposed SAR damage mapping method and outline how it could be deployed in disaster response scenarios.

The problem of RNN over-fitting due to the correlated nature of coherence time series in a single region could potentially be ameliorated by simultaneously training on a large number of coherence time series drawn from areas all over the planet displaying very different temporal behaviors. Furthermore, including additional training features such as the spatial and temporal baseline and the amount of precipitation between sequential SAR acquisitions might allow the network to learn the dependence on additional physical parameters relevant to coherence, thus improving its forecast. The ability to learn from many different input features without a physical model is a key advantage of the deep learning approach.

The work presented here has been using C-band (5.6 cm wavelength) SAR data. As coherence is sensitive to surface disruptions on the scale of the radar wavelength, it could be that we are picking up many false positives caused by superficial damage. Investigating the same disasters with 24 cm wavelength L-band data may provide damage maps that are less prone to pick up small surface disturbances. Unfortunately, dense time series of L-band SAR data are not easily available, although the future launches of L-band SAR satellites (e.g., NISAR Sharma (2019) and ALOS-4 Motohka et al. (2019)) will allow for further exploitation of L-band SAR data for damage mapping. NISAR will also image selected regions using S-band radar, allowing the use of SAR data at multiple wavelengths to further increase the ability of the damage map to distinguish different types of surface change.

Chapter 4

EXPLORING THE EFFECT OF THERMAL PRESSURIZATION ON EARTHQUAKE PROPAGATION THROUGH A CREEPING FAULT USING SIMPLIFIED 2-D MODELS

4.1 Introduction

Faults accommodate strain via rapid slip during earthquakes, or slow slip, known as creep (Avouac, 2015; Burgmann, 2000; Simons et al., 2011). Based on long-term geodetic observations, faults are often divided into locked and creeping sections, with their behavior explained by the frictional properties of each section (Harris, 2017). Locked sections are thought to have velocity-weakening friction, which promotes a stick-slip response to loading. Creeping sections, on the other hand, can be modeled as having velocity-strengthening friction, allowing stress to be accommodated via gradual creep, rather than dynamic rupture. Within this framework, creeping sections of faults represent barriers to earthquake rupture. Properly classifying faults as locked or creeping can therefore allow the possible locations and magnitudes of future earthquakes to be estimated (Kaneko et al., 2010).

The idea that creeping faults represent barriers to earthquake rupture has been challenged by evidence that faults can dramatically weaken at high slip rates (Di Toro et al., 2011; Tsutsumi & Shimamoto, 1997; Tullis, 2007), potentially allowing a fault to exhibit both creep due to velocity-strengthening behavior at slow slip rates, and rapid dynamic failure. One proposed dynamic weakening mechanism is thermal pressurization of pore fluids (Lachenbruch & Sass, 1980; Mase & Smith, 1987; Rice, 2006; Sibson, 1973), whereby rapid fault slip at high stresses generates heat, which in turn raises the pressure of fluids infiltrating the fault zone. This increase in pressure reduces the effective normal stress on the fault, resulting in a decrease in fault strength. Evidence from lab experiments (Badt et al., 2020; Faulkner et al., 2011; French et al., 2014), direct observations of fault zones (Kuo et al., 2022; Ujiie et al., 2010), seismological observations (Viesca & Garagash, 2015), computational models (Cubas et al., 2015; Noda & Lapusta, 2013), and theory (Lachenbruch, 1980; Mase & Smith, 1987; Rice, 2006; Sibson, 1973) suggests that thermal pressurization (TP) can play a significant role in weakening natural faults at high slip rates, and can allow dynamic ruptures to propagate into creeping sections. A variety of processes other than TP have been proposed that would lead to substantial decreases in fault strength during sliding. These include flash heating, gel lubrication, nanoparticle lubrication, decarbonation, dehydration, and fault melting (Di Toro et al., 2011); however, we focus on TP in this work.

The efficiency of TP depends on numerous factors, including the rate of heat generation in the fault zone, the coupling between pore fluid temperature and pressure changes, and the time scales of diffusion of heat and fluid out of the fault zone. A slow rate of heat generation, or rapid diffusion of pore fluid pressure, can result in TP playing a limited role, while the generation and maintenance of high temperatures and pressures can rapidly reduce fault strength (e.g., Lachenbruch (1980) and Rice (2006)). Many of the parameters governing TP are highly uncertain, and can vary in space and time (Aben et al., 2020; Rice, 2006). This uncertainty makes predicting when TP would occur a challenging prospect, leading to significant uncertainties in understanding the behavior of creeping faults when interacting with dynamic ruptures.

The San Andreas Fault (SAF) in California (USA) exhibits both stick-slip and creeping behavior. A long creeping section stretches for around 140 km, from the town of Parkfield in the south to San Juan Baptista in the north (Scott et al., 2020), and is bounded by locked sections to the north and south which have hosted large earthquakes. At the southern end, the transition zone between locked and creeping segments has hosted repeated M_w 6 earthquakes (Bakun et al., 2005; Bakun & Lindh, 1985) and has been the site of intensive study, including direct drilling in to the creeping fault as part of the San Andreas Fault Observatory at Depth (SAFOD) project (Lockner et al., 2011).

The creeping section has not hosted a major earthquake historically, and paleoseismic studies do not show evidence of a major rupture within the past 5000 years (Toké et al., 2011; Toké et al., 2006; Toké & Arrowsmith, 2015). However, geodetic measurements indicate a slip deficit within the creeping section (Jolivet et al., 2015; Maurer & Johnson, 2014) that could potentially be released by seismic slip. French et al. (2014) found that the material from the creeping fault zone at SAFOD could dramatically weaken at seismic slip rates, providing a possible mechanism for ruptures to propagate into the creeping segment. Their results were consistent with TP playing a significant role in the weakening. Recent results by Coffey et al. (2022) present evidence of repeated dynamic ruptures within the creeping section, based on the use of biomarker thermal maturity to calculate previous temperature rises from SAFOD samples. They calculated temperature rises of between 570-1100 °C within a zone that they estimated to have hosted more than 100 earthquakes.

Motivated by these observations, we seek to understand the role that TP can play in allowing earthquakes to rupture the creeping section of the SAF. We construct a highly simplified 2-D model of the fault, centered around Parkfield, with a creeping section that exhibits stable, velocity-strengthening behavior at slow slip rates but can undergo dramatic co-seismic weakening due to TP. We nucleate events on a nearby velocity-weakening patch, then explore how these dynamic ruptures interact with the creeping section as we vary the efficiency of TP. We use a computational methodology that allows us to efficiently model decades-long periods of creep, followed by rapid dynamic ruptures in the presence of TP (Lapusta et al., 2000; Noda & Lapusta, 2010).

Parameters controlling TP are often determined by laboratory measurements (e.g., Tanikawa and Shimamoto (2009) and Wibberley and Shimamoto (2003)), and are then used in simulations (e.g., Cubas et al. (2015) and Noda and Lapusta (2013)). However, several of the parameters controlling TP are uncertain, and can potentially vary substantially during the rupture process (e.g., Aben et al. (2020), Badt et al. (2020), and Brantut and Mitchell (2018)). In this study, we focus on three of the parameters that are least well constrained: the width of the shearing zone, the hydraulic diffusivity, and the coupling coefficient between temperature rise and pressure rise. Proposed values span several orders of magnitude, and we draw on published results to determine the ranges for each parameter. We use these parameters to vary the strength of TP within the creeping zone.

We begin by modeling events in the style of the 2004 M_w 6 Parkfield earthquake. This rupture rapidly arrested in the creeping section of the SAF (Barbot et al., 2012), and we use this observation to rule out the parameter choices for which TP allows a M_w 6-style rupture to propagate substantially into the creeping section. We then simulate larger events, in the style of a hypothetical future M_w 7 rupture on the Cholame segment of the SAF, and observe how they interact with the creeping section. We find a range of physically reasonable TP parameters for which M_w 6-style events rapidly arrest, but M_w 7-style events propagate partially or totally through our simulated creeping section, allowing the event to grow much larger. We also present some simple analytical models that give further insight into the conditions which allow for the creeping section to be ruptured, and discuss the limitations of our simulations.

4.2 Methods

We apply the computational methods developed by Lapusta et al. (2000) and Noda and Lapusta (2010) to simulate long sequences of inter-seismic slip, followed by earthquake nucleation, propagation, and arrest. In order to efficiently explore a wide parameter space, we limit our study to ruptures propagating along a one-dimensional (1-D) fault embedded in a 2-D linear elastic isotropic medium. To approximate the effects of a finite width of the seismogenic zone on a strike-slip fault, we adopt a crustal plane model (Kaneko & Lapusta, 2008; Lapusta, 2001; Lehner et al., 1981). The only non-zero component of slip is along-strike, averaged over the assumed depth of the fault, H_{seis}. Below H_{seis}, the medium is coupled to a substrate moving at the loading rate, v_{pl}. The parameters we adopt in this study are given in Table 4.1, and further description is given in Section 4.2.4.

4.2.1 Rate-and-State Friction

We model the shear resistance of the fault as the product of the effective normal stress and the friction coefficient given by the standard laboratory-derived rate-and-state law (Dieterich, 1978; Ruina, 1983): :

$$\tau = \sigma_{eff} f(v, \theta) \tag{4.1}$$

$$= (\sigma - p) \left[f^* + a \log\left(\frac{v}{V^*}\right) + b \log\left(\frac{\theta v^*}{D_{RS}}\right) \right], \tag{4.2}$$

where τ is the shear strength which is equal to the shear stress, σ_{eff} ($= \sigma - p$) is the Terzaghi effective stress, σ is the normal stress, p is the pore fluid pressure, f is the rate-and-state friction coefficient, v is the sliding velocity, f^* is the reference friction coefficient, defined as the steady state value of f when sliding at the reference velocity V^*, D_{RS} is the characteristic slip for the evolution of the state variable, and a and b are the rate-and-state constitutive parameters.

The evolution of the state variable, θ, is given by the aging law:

$$\dot{\theta} = 1 - \frac{v\theta}{D_{RS}}. \tag{4.3}$$

At steady state, $\dot{\theta} = 0$ and the friction coefficient reduces to:

$$f_{ss}(v) = f^* + (a - b) \log\left(\frac{v}{V^*}\right). \tag{4.4}$$

Equation 4.4 shows that the steady-state friction is governed by the sliding velocity v and the parameter $(a - b)$. When $(a - b) > 0$, friction increases with sliding velocity, a situation known as velocity strengthening. Velocity strengthening results in stable sliding when a steady load is applied. Patches with $(a - b) < 0$ are referred to as velocity weakening, and can potentially nucleate seismic ruptures (e.g., Rice and Ruina (1983) and Rubin and Ampuero (2005)).

4.2.2 Enhanced Dynamic Weakening via TP

To simulate the evolution of temperature due to shear heating and the resulting changes in pore fluid pressure, we use the following two coupled partial differential equations (Noda & Lapusta, 2010):

$$\frac{\partial T}{\partial t} = \alpha_{th}\frac{\partial^2 T}{\partial y^2} + \frac{\tau v}{\rho c}\frac{\exp(-y^2/2w^2)}{\sqrt{2\pi}w}, \tag{4.5}$$

$$\frac{\partial p}{\partial t} = \alpha_{hy}\frac{\partial^2 p}{\partial y^2} + \Lambda\frac{\partial T}{\partial t}, \tag{4.6}$$

where T is the temperature, α_{th} is the thermal diffusivity, τ is the shear stress on the fault, v is the sliding velocity, ρc is the specific heat, p is the pore fluid pressure, α_{hy} is the hydraulic diffusivity, and Λ is the coupling coefficient that gives the change in pore pressure for a given change in temperature under undrained conditions. We assume a Gaussian distribution of the shearing rate, with w being the root-mean-square half-width of the shear-rate distribution and y being the perpendicular distance from the fault.

4.2.3 Model Setup

Our model is designed as a highly simplified representation of the southern portion of the creeping section of the SAF, and the locked Cholame segment, centered around the town of Parkfield, California. At Parkfield, the fault transitions from locked in the south, to the creeping segment in the north. This transition zone has hosted repeated M_w 6 earthquakes over the last century (Bakun et al., 2005; Bakun & Lindh, 1985).

We draw on the work of Barbot et al. (2012) in constructing a 2-D model consisting of a velocity-weakening patch with velocity-strengthening segments on either side. When loaded, these velocity-strengthening sections creep at the plate rate, set at 23 mm/yr based on observed creep rates (Titus, 2006). This creep loads the velocity-weakening patch, causing dynamic ruptures to nucleate. We put a small initial stress perturbation near the right-hand edge of the velocity-weakening patch, which results in the events nucleating from the right and propagating to the left, where they hit the creeping section (Figure 4.1). Our model setup gives a total length of the creeping section of around 80 km. While this is shorter than the creeping section of the SAF, in practice this makes little difference to our results and reduces the computational burden. The velocity-strengthening patch on the right-hand side of the model is similar to the modeling approach used by Barbot et al. (2012). It allows the velocity-weakening patch to be loaded from the right-hand side in order to create ruptures that propagate to the left. However, the patch does not directly relate to observed creep rates on the SAF, which decrease rapidly to the south of Parkfield. We note that our goal is to focus on the impact of variable TP efficiency in the creeping section, and not to realistically model the potentially complex transition zone around Parkfield (e.g., Simpson et al. (2006)).

We seek to understand the response of the creeping section to the incoming ruptures of different sizes as the efficiency of TP varies. TP parameters are constant throughout the left-hand side creeping section, with no TP in other regions ($\Lambda = 0$ MPa/K). In our simulations, we create incoming ruptures of two different styles. The first type of rupture is designed to be similar to the 2004 M_w 6 Parkfield event. We use the observation that this event rapidly arrested in the creeping section to place constraints on the efficiency of TP. We also simulate a larger event, with a magnitude of around M_w 7 in the absence of TP. To control the event size, we vary two parameters: the length of the velocity-weakening patch, λ_{vw}, and the crustal plane width, H_{seis}. We determine the approximate event sizes by examining the rupture behaviour in the absence of TP, where the rupture is constrained to the velocity-weakening patch. In Figure 4.1, we illustrate our model setup and slip profiles for the two styles of events, and describe them in more detail below.

The crustal plane model is used to approximate the depth-averaged slip over the seismogenic fault depth H_{seis}, with the fault loaded at v_{pl} at the bottom, and a free surface at the top (Lapusta, 2001; Lehner et al., 1981). H_{seis} can also be regarded at the half-width of a fault that is constrained to move at v_{pl} from the bottom and the top, with no free surface. This situation is more akin to the 2004 Parkfield earthquake, which was predominantly confined to below 5-km depth and did not rupture to the surface (e.g., Barbot et al. (2012)).

For the M_w 6-style events, we base our geometry on the inferred rupture parameters for the M_w 6 2004 Parkfield earthquake. This event propagated to the north, rupturing a patch roughly 25 km long by 4 km wide, and rapidly arrested in the creeping section (e.g., Barbot et al. (2012)). We create a velocity-weakening patch 25 km long, and set the crustal plane thickness, H_{seis}, to 2 km, or half of the inferred rupture patch width. This model setup effectively constrains ruptures to a 4-km wide patch along the entire length of the fault. In reality, in situations where TP allowed ruptures to propagate substantially into the creeping section, the rupture would likely expand over more of the fault depth. This artificial constraint on the depth extent of the ruptures acts to inhibit propagation into the creeping section for the M_w 6-style events.

For the M_w 6-style events, our choice of frictional parameters results in slip of around 66 cm along most of the velocity-weakening patch (Figure 4.1(a)). This number is consistent with the maximum slip, found at around 7 km depth, in the kinematic inversions and simulations of Barbot et al. (2012), although is larger than that found by some other authors (e.g., Johanson et al. (2006) and Langbein et al. (2006)). The use of the crustal plane model means that the slip in our model is the average over the depth of the patch, so the magnitude of our events is somewhat larger than the observed M_w 6; however, this difference should not significantly affect our conclusions.

For the M_w 7-style events, we extend the velocity-weakening patch to be 80 km long, and set the seismogenic depth to be larger, $H_{seis} = 8$ km, resulting in ruptures with slip of around 2.2 m along most of the velocity-weakening patch. H_{seis} is here used to represent the full depth of the rupture, which is assumed to span from the surface to a depth of 8 km. These parameters are not directly based on observational constraints, but are designed to produce an intermediate size of event, larger than the M_w 6-style, but still much smaller than the M 7.7 1857 Fort Tejon earthquake (e.g., Zielke et al. (2012)), the most recent major earthquake to rupture the SAF near Parkfield. Note that the Fort Tejon event likely nucleated around the Parkfield transition zone, then propagated from the north to the south (Sieh, 1978a), unlike the ruptures in our simulations.

4.2.4 Parameters Controlling TP

Equations 4.2, 4.5, and 4.6 describe a coupled system whereby the shear stress controls the rate of heat production, which in turn governs the evolution of pore pressure, which feeds back into the shear stress via the effective normal stress. In order for TP of pore fluids to occur, there must be sufficient heat generated to increase the pore fluid pressure, and this heat and pressure must remain sufficiently confined to the shearing layer over the time scales of seismic slip. The relative weight of these processes is controlled by the thermal and hydraulic diffusivities α_{th} and α_{hy}, specific heat ρc, fault zone half-width w, and coupling coefficient Λ. Of these parameters, the values of $\alpha_{th} = 10^{-6}$ m^2/s and $\rho c = 2.7$ MPa/K are relatively well constrained from laboratory results and have been used in previous computational work (e.g., Noda and Lapusta (2010, 2013), Rice (2006), and Wibberley and Shimamoto (2005)).

We therefore focus our attention on Λ, α_{hy}, and w. Given these parameters are uncertain, we search the literature for the range of values proposed for each of these quantities, and explore that range in our simulations. We assume that each parameter is fixed during each simulation, which may not be the case in reality (see Section 4.5.2). Exploring the effects of potential evolution of these quantities during rupture should be the subject of future work.

The coupling coefficient, Λ, depends on the degree of damage to the fault gouge material, and also evolves with the pressure-temperature conditions. Rice (2006) draws on experimental results (including from gouge drawn from the Median Tectonic Line, Japan, presented by Wibberley and Shimamoto (2003)) to suggest values between 0.31 and 0.98 MPa/K, with higher damage resulting in lower values and thus less efficient TP. Noda and Lapusta (2013) calculate values of 0.036 and 0.069 MPa/K based on laboratory measurements from Tanikawa and Shimamoto (2009) of material taken from different points in the Chelungpu fault zone, Taiwan. Aben et al. (2020) give values in the range 0-2 MPa/K depending on the depth and degree of damage. In our work, we vary Λ over the range from 0.01 MPa/K to 1 MPa/K. Most of these values would be appropriate for the fault with off-fault damage due to the rupture, with the simulations essentially ignoring the transition from undamaged to damaged conditions and considering the values for the damaged fault.

The hydraulic diffusivity, α_{hy}, also depends on the degree of damage and the pressure-temperature conditions. Rice (2006) gives values between $0.86 - 6.04 \times 10^{-6}$ m^2/s, with higher damage resulting in larger hydraulic diffusivities. Noda and Lapusta (2013) calculate values of 3.5×10^{-2} and 7.0×10^{-5} m^2/s, again based on the results of two different samples presented by Tanikawa and Shimamoto (2009). Aben et al. (2020) gives a wide range of parameters, from $\sim 10^{-8}$ to 10^{-2} m^2/s, depending on the depth and degree of damage. For our work, we vary the hydraulic diffusivity over the range 10^{-5} to 10^{-2} m^2/s.

Theoretical, observational, and experimental results can be used to place bounds on the half-width w of the shearing zone during seismic slip. Field observations of faults often find broad zones of damage, on the scale of meters, surrounding narrow zones of ultracataclasite and fault gouge, centimeters to millimeters wide, which host earthquake slip (e.g., Mitchell and Faulkner (2009) and Sibson (2003)). Microstructural analysis indicates that, within these narrow zones, slip can be accommodated over narrower "principle slip zones," on the order of 0.1 to 1 mm thick (e.g., Chester and Chester (1998), De Paola et al. (2008), and Heermance et al. (2003)). Rice et al. (2014) and Platt et al. (2014) argued that fault gouge at seismogenic depths would tend to undergo extreme shear localization, resulting in shear being accommodated over zones 5-40 μm wide. Coffey et al. (2022) examined material drawn directly from the SAFOD bore hole in the creeping section of the SAF, finding multiple slip layers with thicknesses between 100 μm and 1.8 cm, with an average of 2 mm. To encapsulate the broad range of the proposed shear-zone widths, we vary the half-width, w, from 0.01 mm (10 μm) to 100 mm. These values remain constant during slip; however, we acknowledge that the wider shearing layers may be unstable, and localize, over extended slip (Platt et al., 2014; Rice et al., 2014).

We set the initial effective normal stress, σ_{eff}, at 120 MPa, the approximate value at 7 km depth with hydrostatic pore pressure. Based on experimental results from material obtained from SAFOD we choose $f^* = 0.15$ within the creeping section (Lockner et al., 2011). The steady-state velocity dependence of the rate-and-state friction is governed by the quantity $\sigma_{eff}(a - b)$ (Equation 4.4), which we set to 0.48 MPa within the creeping section, consistent with values determined from inversions of post-seismic slip (Barbot et al., 2009; Barbot et al., 2012; Chang et al., 2013) and experimental measurements of fault properties (Lockner et al., 2011). Properties within the velocity-weakening section are chosen to give events of the desired size, as discussed by Barbot et al. (2012). All parameters are given in Table 4.1.

The dramatic weakening caused by TP can lead to very rapid increases in slip rates, resulting in high strain rates. In reality, such high strain rates would lead to inelastic yielding, i.e. damage, off the fault around the rupture front. Such behavior can be approximated by imposing a slip velocity limit that varies with the normal stress (Andrews, 2005; Lambert et al., 2021). We set $v_{lim} = 15$ m/s, to approximate the behavior at roughly 7 km depth.

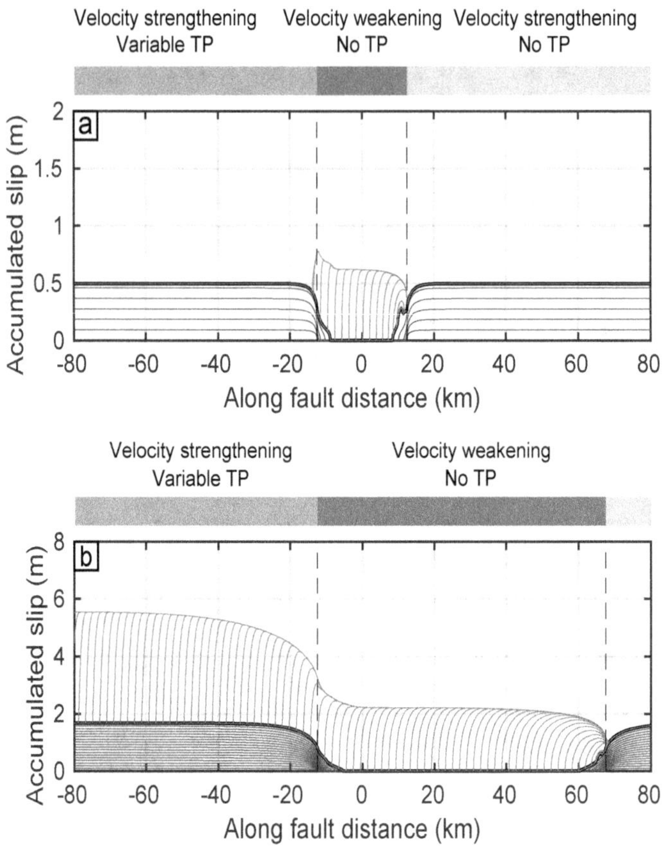

Figure 4.1: Examples of M_w 6 and M_w 7-style events. Blue contours show accumulated inter-seismic slip every four years. Red lines show accumulated co-seismic slip every 0.5 seconds. (a) M_w 6-style event. A 25-km-long velocity-weakening patch is placed between two velocity-strengthening patches, the crustal plane thickness is H_{seis} = 2 km. The velocity-strengthening patch on the left has TP with $\Lambda = 0.34$ MPa/K, w = 10 mm and $\alpha_{hy} = 10^{-4}$ m^2/s for this case; the parameters are varied in other simulations (Table 4.1). The TP with these parameters is not efficient enough for the M_w 6-style event to propagate into the creeping section. (b) M_w 7-style event. The velocity-weakening patch is expanded to 80 km long, and crustal plane thickness increased to H_{seis} = 8 km. TP parameters have the same values as in (a). The larger event now activates sufficient TP to propagate through the creeping section and hit the boundary of our model (not shown here), allowing the event to grow well beyond M_w 7.

4.2.5 Example of Simulated Rupture in the Creeping Section

In Figure 4.1(b), we illustrated a M_W 7-style event propagating through the creeping section due to TP. In Figure 4.2, we also show the evolution of the physical parameters at a point on the edge of the creeping section during a period of creep, followed by a M_W 7-style event that propagates into the creeping section. Figure 4.2(a) shows the evolution of shear stress: steady creep occurs at a background stress set by the rate-and-state parameters, before seismic slip creates a spike to a peak stress and rapid evolution to a higher stress level, again controlled by the rate-and-state parameters (the evolution of the state parameter is shown in Figure 4.2(e)). Without TP, this increase in shear stress would rapidly arrest the ruptures. However, TP causes shear stress to decay exponentially with slip, due to the reduction in effective normal stress (Figure 4.2(b)). The dramatic reduction in stress allows several meters of slip to accumulate with temperature change limited to 370 °C (Figure 4.2(d)).

4.3 Analytical Models of Thermal Pressurization

4.3.1 TP Weakening Length Scales

Previous authors have derived analytical solutions for the evolution of stress due to TP (Lachenbruch, 1980; Mase & Smith, 1987; Rice, 2006). These models allow us to gain some insight into how TP parameters may control the rupture of the creeping section. Two end-member solutions have been derived, one for constant velocity slip on a plane, in which the very existence of the solution is crucially dependent on the off-fault diffusion of heat and fluids, and the other for adiabatic, undrained shear over a zone of finite width, which is only valid if the layer is wide enough for the heat and fluid diffusion to be negligible for the duration of the event.

For slip on a plane (i.e. the case with an infinitely thin shear zone), one has (Mase & Smith, 1987; Rice, 2006):

$$\tau = f(\sigma_n - p_o) \exp\left(\frac{\delta}{L^*}\right) \operatorname{erfc}\left(\sqrt{\frac{\delta}{L^*}}\right), \tag{4.7}$$

where:

$$L^* = 4\left(\frac{\rho c}{f\Lambda}\right)^2 \frac{(\sqrt{\alpha_{hy}} + \sqrt{\alpha_{th}})^2}{v_{seis}}, \tag{4.8}$$

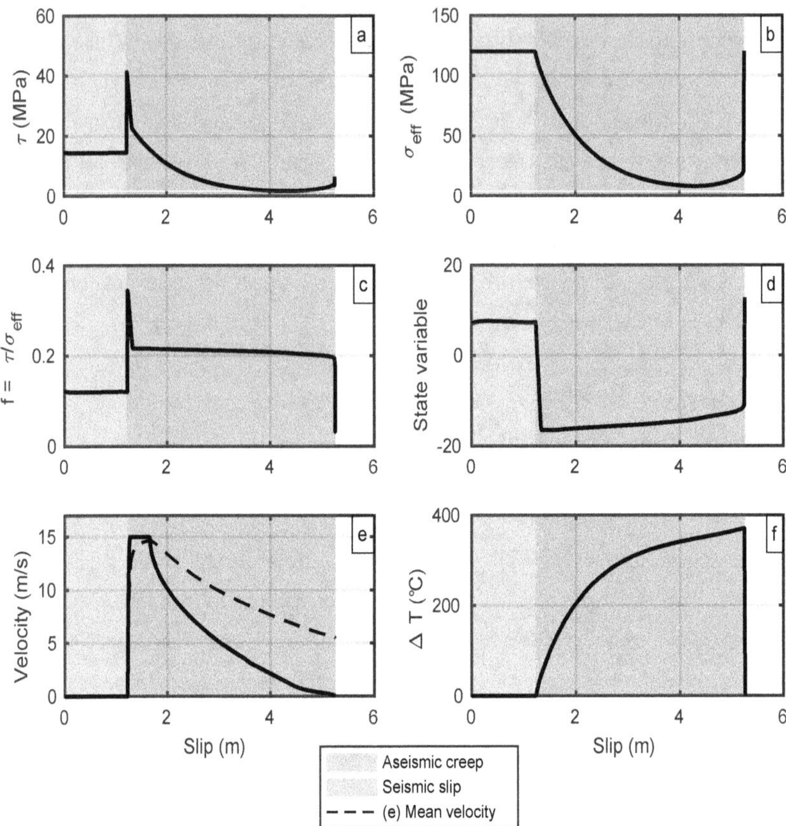

Figure 4.2: Evolution of parameters with slip for a point within the creeping section (position -15 km) during a M_w 7-style event that fully ruptures the creeping section. TP parameters are Λ = 0.34 MPa/K, w = 10 mm, and α_{hy} = 10^{-5} m^2/s. **(a)** Shear stress (τ) with slip. **(b)** Effective normal stress (σ_{eff}) with slip. **(c)** Coefficient of friction (τ/σ_{eff}) with slip. **(d)** State variable term ($\ln[V^*\theta/D_{RS}]$) with slip. **(e)** Slip velocity with slip. The dashed line indicates the mean slip velocity since the start of the event. Note the 15 m/s slip velocity limit. **(f)** Temperature change with slip.

and v_{seis} is the representative seismic slip rate, f is the representative dynamic friction coefficient (both assumed constant), δ is the accumulating slip, p_0 is the ambient pore fluid pressure, and the other quantities are as defined above.

The case of adiabatic, undrained shear over the zone of width h gives (Lachenbruch, 1980):

$$\tau = f(\sigma - p_o) \exp\left(-\frac{\delta}{\delta_c}\right), \tag{4.9}$$

where:

$$\delta_c = \frac{\rho c h}{f \Lambda}. \tag{4.10}$$

Note that this solution assumes that shearing is uniformly distributed over the layer of thickness h, compared to our simulations which use a Gaussian distribution of shear rate with root-mean-square half-width w. We assume the approximation $h = w$ when evaluating δ_c for our simulations.

4.3.2 Estimating When TP Allows Propagation Through the Creeping Section

If slip propagates into the creeping section, there would be an initial increase in stress due to the velocity-strengthening properties of the fault, potentially followed by weakening due to TP (Figure 4.3). To estimate the conditions under which TP would allow an event to rupture the creeping section, we estimate the slip required for TP to overcome the velocity-strengthening effect and cause a positive stress drop (Noda & Lapusta, 2013). For a point in the creeping section, undergoing stable creep at the plate rate, v_{pl}, its initial stress τ_{creep} is set by the rate-and-state friction properties of the interface:

$$\tau_{creep} = \sigma_{eff} \left[f^* + (a - b) \ln\left(\frac{v_{pl}}{V^*}\right) \right]. \tag{4.11}$$

The incoming rupture would initially cause the stress to jump to a peak value, the so-called "direct effect" of rate-and-state friction (e.g., Scholz (1998)). Assuming a representative seismic slip velocity, v_{seis}, is supported for a sufficient amount of slip (see Equation 4.21) due to incoming dynamic loading, this stress would then evolve to its steady-state value, τ_{seis}:

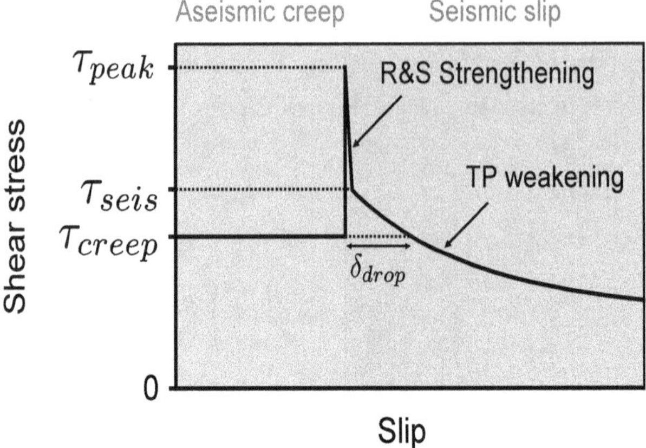

Figure 4.3: Schematic evolution of shear stress, τ, with slip for a point in the creeping section of the fault that experiences TP due to incoming dynamic rupture. The quantities illustrated are used in the theoretical estimates of Section 4.3.1. Steady aseismic creep happens with the slip velocity v_{pl} and stress τ_{creep}. When an event propagates into the creeping section, there is an initial rapid increase of stress to τ_{peak} (the rate-and-state direct effect) and then a decay to τ_{seis}, controlled by the steady-state rate-and-state parameter. TP can then be activated due to the resulting shear heating, causing the stress to continue to decrease. Given sufficient slip before the rupture arrests, the stress could decrease back to τ_{creep} over a slip of δ_{drop}, and then even below this level, allowing for a positive stress drop in the creeping section. A simulation output of this evolution can be seen in Figure 4.2(a).

$$\tau_{seis} = \sigma_{eff} \left[f^* + (a - b) \ln \left(\frac{v_{seis}}{V^*} \right) \right]. \tag{4.12}$$

The length scale of evolution to steady-state is controlled by the rate-and-state critical slip distance, D_{RS}, which is set to 4 mm for our simulations. This value is large compared to laboratory results, but values on this scale are often used in computational work to make the problem tractable (e.g., Barbot et al. (2012), Erickson et al. (2020), and Noda and Lapusta (2013)). Smaller values of D_{RS} would promote rupture, since the slip needed to evolve the shear stress from the larger direct-effect peak to the smaller steady-state seismic resistance would be lower. When applying the slip-on-a-plane and adiabatic, undrained theoretical solutions given above, we assume both a constant seismic slip velocity and a constant friction coefficient over length scales relevant for TP. These assumptions imply that rate-and-state evolution occurs much faster than TP, which we analyse further in Section 4.5.3.

A necessary condition to sustain the rupture in the creeping section is to achieve a positive dynamic stress drop. Given the velocity-strengthening properties of this part of the fault the shear stress is greater when sliding and seismic rates ($\tau_{seis} > \tau_{creep}$), and TP must lower the stress to below τ_{creep} for the stress drop to be positive. The amount of slip required for such stress evolution, δ_{drop}, can be estimated from the analytical solutions presented in Section 4.3.1. We define $\delta_{drop}^{(c)}$ as the estimate of δ_{drop} assuming adiabatic, undrained conditions, and δ_{drop}^{*} as the estimate assuming slip on a plane. For the adiabatic, undrained solution, the slip for a positive stress drop, δ_{drop} can be derived from Equation 4.9:

$$\delta_{drop}^{(c)} = \delta_c \ln\left(\frac{\tau_{seis}}{\tau_{creep}}\right). \tag{4.13}$$

For the slip-on-a-plane solution, Equation 4.7 gives us an expression for required slip:

$$\exp\left(\frac{\delta_{drop}^{*}}{L^{*}}\right) \mathrm{erfc}\left(\sqrt{\frac{\delta_{drop}^{*}}{L^{*}}}\right) = \frac{\tau_{creep}}{\tau_{seis}}, \tag{4.14}$$

which can be solved numerically.

To calculate τ_{seis} and δ_{drop}^{*}, we must choose a seismic slip rate that is representative for a point on the edge of the creeping section over the slip range δ_{drop}. At a point within the velocity-weakening patch, but close to the creeping section, our simulations give an average slip velocity slightly greater than 6 m/s over the entire event for both the M_w 6 and M_w 7-style events. Based on these averages, we choose $v_{seis} = 6$ m/s. We provide further discussion of this value in Section 4.5. For our chosen velocity-strengthening rate-and-state parameters (Table 4.1), and $v_{seis} = 6$ m/s, $\tau_{creep} \approx 15$ MPa, $\tau_{seis} \approx 25$ MPa, and we can calculate $\delta_{drop}^{(c)} \approx 0.53\delta_c$ and $\delta_{drop}^{*} \approx 0.30L^{*}$.

4.3.3 The Transition Between Adiabatic, Undrained Solutions and Slip-on-a-Plane Solutions

Our simulated faults have finite widths and non-zero diffusivities, so are never truly in the slip-on-a-plane or adiabatic/undrained regimes. We therefore need to consider the circumstances under which each of these models would be a useful approximation to the full solution. The adiabatic, undrained case would be most applicable when the diffusion length scales are small compared with the width of the fault for the duration of seismic slip. The slip-on-a-plane solution would be most applicable when the diffusion length scales are large with respect to the fault width (Rempel & Rice, 2006).

Garagash (2012) and Viesca and Garagash (2015) define a lumped hydrothermal diffusivity, $\alpha = (\sqrt{\alpha_{hy}} + \sqrt{\alpha_{th}})^2$, which they use to calculate a length scale for hydrothermal diffusion, $l_d = \sqrt{4\alpha t}$. From this length scale, they derive a hydrothermal diffusion timescale, the time at which the hydrothermal diffusion length scale is equal to the fault zone width: $t_d = h^2/(4\alpha)$.

Assuming that the fault slips at a constant rate v_{seis}, the distance slipped during the diffusion timescale would be $\delta_d = v_{seis} t_d$. Taking the definition of t_d, L^* and δ_c from above, Viesca and Garagash (2015) derived a relationship for the δ_d in terms of the weakening length scales δ_c and L^*:

$$\delta_d = \frac{\delta_c^2}{L^*}, \tag{4.15}$$

which can also be expressed directly in terms of fault zone parameters as:

$$\delta_d = \frac{h^2 v_{seis}}{4\alpha}. \tag{4.16}$$

This consideration implies that, for slip $\delta \ll \delta_c^2/L^*$, the diffusive length scale would be small compared with the fault width, so the shear zone would be in the adiabatic, undrained regime. $\delta \gg \delta_c^2/L^*$ implies that the diffusive length scale is much wider than the fault zone, making the slip-on-a-plane solution the better approximation.

For our parameter combinations, the hydraulic diffusivity varies over several orders of magnitude, and is at least an order of magnitude greater than the thermal diffusivity, resulting in the lumped hydrothermal diffusivity being approximately equal to hydraulic diffusivity. δ_d therefore is best used to determine the slip at which fluid diffusion reaches the scale of the fault width, i.e. the boundary between undrained and drained models. The smaller value of thermal diffusivity means that greater slip than δ_d would be required before thermal diffusion reaches the scale of the fault width and the slip can no longer be approximated as adiabatic. This slip can be estimated from the expression $\delta_{d,th} = (\delta_c^2/L^*)(\alpha/\alpha_{th})$. In this work, we are primarily interested in the variation in fault strength, which is governed directly by the evolution of pore fluid pressure. As δ_d approximately determines the transition from undrained to drained behavior, we use this value to determine which end-member model best determines the evolution of pore fluid pressure, and thus fault strength, ignoring the fact that this is not the same as the adiabatic boundary. See Section 3.1 of Rice (2006), as well as Rempel and Rice (2006), for more discussion of this issue.

To determine which end-member model of TP best approximates the behavior over the slip required for a positive stress drop, δ_{drop}, we compare the diffusive length scale δ_d (Equation 4.15) to the relevant expression for δ_{drop}, which depends on the chosen model. For the adiabatic, undrained case, we have:

$$\frac{\delta_d}{\delta_{drop}^{(c)}} \approx 1.90\left(\frac{\delta_c}{L^*}\right) \tag{4.17}$$

$$= 1.90\left(\frac{f\Lambda h v_{seis}}{4\rho c\alpha}\right). \tag{4.18}$$

For the slip-on-a-plane case:

$$\frac{\delta_d}{\delta_{drop}^*} \approx 3.28\left(\frac{\delta_c^2}{L^{*2}}\right) \tag{4.19}$$

$$= 3.28\left(\frac{f\Lambda h v_{seis}}{4\rho c\alpha}\right)^2. \tag{4.20}$$

Note that both expressions contain the same physical parameters. The adiabatic, undrained solution would be a good approximation over the slip length required for a positive stress drop when $\delta_d/\delta_{drop}^{(c)} \gg 1$, i.e. $\delta_c \gg 0.53L^*$. The slip-on-a-plane solution would be a good approximation when $\delta_d/\delta_{drop}^* \ll 1$, i.e $\delta_c \ll 0.55L^*$. Therefore, there is a transition at around $\delta_c \approx L^*/2$ for which solution is a better approximation, but the ratio between δ_d and δ_{drop} scales differently between the two end-member solutions as the physical parameters are varied.

4.4 Rupture Propagation Into the Creeping Section

4.4.1 Simulation results

As we vary the parameters of TP in the velocity-strengthening section, the simulated ruptures span the range from rapidly arresting to propagating through the entire section. In Figures 4.4 and 4.5, we show the fraction of the creeping section that is ruptured for M_w 6 and M_w 7-style events, respectively, as we vary the hydraulic diffusivity (α_{hy}), fault half-width (w), and TP coupling (Λ) over several orders of magnitude. For $\Lambda = 0.01$ MPa/K, there is negligible influence of TP for both event sizes and all combinations of α_{hy} and w within our chosen ranges, and the rupture rapidly dies out due to the velocity-strengthening rate-and-state properties of the creeping section. TP also has negligible effects when $w = 100$ mm. Some enhanced propagation into the creeping section is possible when $\alpha_{hy} = 10^{-2}$ m^2/s, but the creeping section never fully ruptures when the hydraulic diffusivity is this high.

The coupling coefficient of $\Lambda = 0.1$ MPa/K is sufficient to allow M_w 6-style ruptures to propagate several kilometers into the creeping section for the thinnest faults and lowest diffusivities (Figure 4.4(b)). For $\Lambda = 0.34$ and 1 MPa/K, we find numerous parameter combinations for which M_w 6-style events rupture the entire creeping section, resulting in events much larger than M_w 6 (Figure 4.4(c)-(d)). Using the observation that the 2004 M_w 6 Parkfield event arrested in the creeping section, we can rule out these fault models as having overly efficient TP. We mark these parameter combinations with black boxes.

For the M_w 7-style events shown in Figure 4.5, the larger event size results in greater propagation through the creeping section for every parameter combination. For $\Lambda = 0.1$ MPa/K and larger, we find several combinations of parameters for which the M_w 6-style events arrest in the creeping section, but the M_w 7-style events rupture the whole fault. These parameter combinations are highlighted by red boxes. Note we also run simulations for $\Lambda = 0.069$ MPa/K. These results are included in Figures 4.8 and 4.9 but are not plotted in Figures 4.4 or 4.5.

4.4.2 Application of Analytical Models

For each combination of parameters, we use the analytical solutions of Section 4.3.1 to estimate the slip required for TP to give a positive stress drop, δ_{drop}, and compare these values to the fraction of the creeping section ruptured by M_w 7-style events (Figures 4.6(a)-(b) and 4.7(a)-(b)).

We also evaluate δ_d / δ_{drop} for each set of parameters; this ratio allows us to determine whether conditions assumed for the analytical solution are a good approximation to our models (see Section 4.3.3). For the adiabatic, undrained solution to be a good approximation, we need the hydrothermal diffusion length scale to be small in comparison to the fault width over the relevant slip distance, and we set a threshold of $\delta_{drop}^{(c)} < 0.1\delta_d$ (recall that δ_d is the slip required for diffusion scales to be comparable to the fault zone width). For the slip-on-a-plane solution, the approximation should

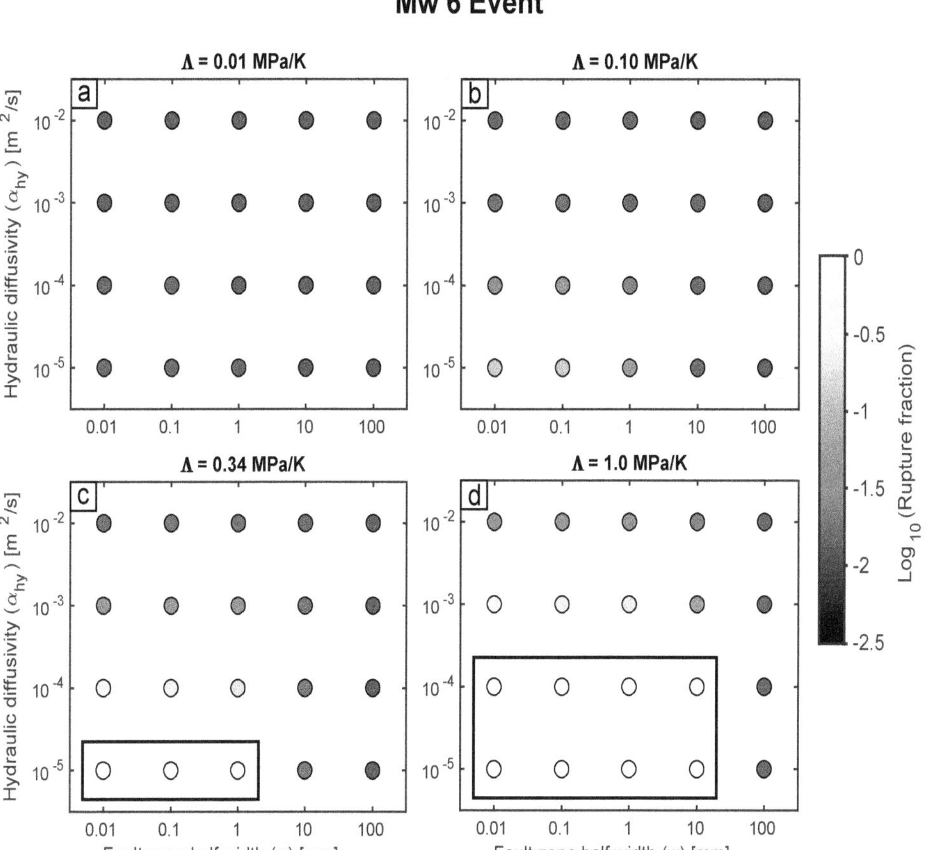

Figure 4.4: Fraction of the creeping section ruptured for a M_w 6-style event and varying TP parameters. The value of the TP coupling coefficient, Λ, increases from (a) to (d), resulting in increasingly efficient TP and greater rupture fractions. Points within black squares are those models for which the event fully ruptures the creeping section, indicating that TP is too efficient to be consistent with the observation of the 2004 M_w 6 event arresting in the creeping section.

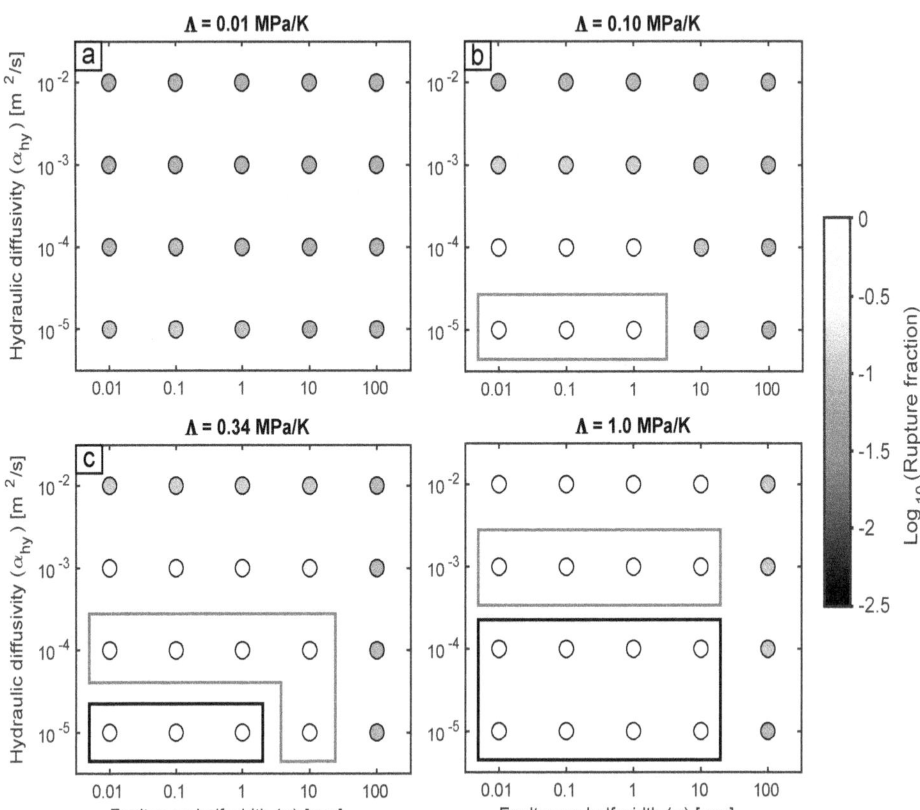

Figure 4.5: Fraction of the creeping section ruptured for a M_w 7-style event and varying TP parameters. The size of the TP coupling coefficient, Λ, increases from (a) to (d), resulting in increasingly efficient TP and greater rupture fractions. Points within black boxes are those that fully ruptured the creeping section for M_w 6-style events (Figure 4.4), indicating that TP is too efficient to be consistent with the observation of the 2004 M_w 6 event arresting in the creeping section. Points within red boxes are those that arrested in the creeping section for M_w 6-style events, but fully rupture the creeping section for M_w 7-style events.

work best for faults that are thin compared to the diffusion lengths, and we require the hydrothermal diffusion length scale to be much larger than the fault width. This condition can be expressed as $\delta^*_{drop} > 10\delta_d$. In Figures 4.6(c)-(d) and 4.7(c)-(d), we use these thresholds of δ_d/δ_{drop} to illustrate the expected validity of the analytical solution, indicating which simulations we expect to be well approximated by the slip-on-a-plane and adiabatic, undrained regimes. For clarity, we shade out areas in Figures 4.6(a)-(b) and 4.7(a)-(b) where the relevant analytical solution is invalid according to our chosen bounds. These plots demonstrate that lower hydraulic diffusivities and larger fault widths move us towards the adiabatic, undrained regime, as they favor the retention of heat and pressure within the fault zone. Increasing the TP coupling coefficient, Λ, shortens the distance δ_{drop}, resulting in less time for hydrothermal diffusion and therefore also shifting us towards the adiabatic, undrained regime (see Equations 4.17 and 4.14).

One would expect that if the dynamic rupture brings a sufficient amount of seismic slip to the velocity-strengthening region, in comparison with δ_{drop}, the associated shear heating could activate TP and allow the rupture to propagate. This is exactly what we observe. Specifically, in Figures 4.6(a)-(b) and 4.7(a)-(b), we highlight the point at which δ_{drop} is equal to the M_w 7 slip (δ_{event}) with a red dashed line. For models that lie within their approximation bounds, this contour marks a transition point for the fraction of the creeping section ruptured. Where $\delta_{event} > \delta_{drop}$, which indicates that the incoming event brings sufficient seismic slip for a positive stress drop from TP, we see a substantial or complete rupture of the creeping section, whereas $\delta_{event} < \delta_{drop}$ results in the events rapidly arresting in the creeping section.

To summarize the outcomes for all combinations of parameters in a single figure, we plot the fraction of the creeping section ruptured by each event against the ratio between the total slip of the incoming rupture pulse without TP, δ_{event}, and the estimated slip required for TP to give a positive stress drop, δ_{drop}. ($\delta_{event} \approx 66$ cm and 2.2 m for the M_w 6 and M_w 7-style events, respectively). We compute δ_{drop} using both the adiabatic, undrained solution ($\delta^{(c)}_{drop}$) and the slip-on-a-plane solution (δ^*_{drop}). We then separate data points with estimates δ_{drop} obtained from analytical models within our chosen bounds, shown in Figure 4.8, and the rest, shown in Figure 4.9.

Figure 4.8 clearly highlights the transition in the fraction of the creeping section ruptured as the total event slip becomes sufficient to create a positive stress drop in the velocity-strengthening region. When $\delta_{event} << \delta_{drop}$, TP is inefficient at overcoming rate-and-state velocity-strengthening properties, and the (small) rupture fraction is determined mainly by the amount of strengthening set by the rate-and-state parameters. As the M_w 7 rupture brings more slip than the M_w 6 event, it can propagate a longer distance into the creeping section without TP, resulting in a larger minimum rupture fraction. Between $\delta_{event} = \delta_{drop}$ and $\delta_{event} = 10\delta_{drop}$, the simulations give at least partial ruptures of the creeping section (most in the range of 10-50%), and for $\delta_{event} > 10\delta_{drop}$ all simulations rupture the entire creeping section.

Figure 4.9 shows that estimates of δ_{drop} based on less relevant analytical models do an overall poor job of estimating when the creeping section would be ruptured. The adiabatic, undrained solution neglects the transport of heat and fluid out of the fault zone, and therefore gives the upper limit on the efficiency of TP for each combination of parameters. The adiabatic, undrained analytical approach applied to conditions where diffusion is significant, i.e. $\dot{\delta}_{drop}^{(c)} > \delta_d$, often suggests that the creeping section should be fully ruptured (i.e. $\delta_{event} >> \delta_{drop}^{(c)}$) when this is not observed, as can be seen for the large number of points in the bottom right of the plots in Figure 4.9. Similarly, when the slip-on-a-plane solution is applied to conditions for which $\delta_{drop} < \delta_d$, the finite width of the fault zone results in more distributed heat generation and thus less efficient TP than the solution predicts. The symbols with white fill represent approximations of δ_{drop} that can still be good, just somewhat outside the bounds established earlier, and some of them may belong in Figure 4.8.

To study the validity bounds of each approximation (rather than assuming factors of 10 as done so far), we can compare the analytical estimates of δ_{drop} with its values from our simulations. This is the direction of ongoing work.

4.4.3 Summary of Expressions

Summarizing the expressions defined above, we have the slip-on-a-plane and adiabatic, undrained TP weakening length scales (Equations 4.8 and 4.10):

$$L^* = 4\left(\frac{\rho c}{f\Lambda}\right)^2 \frac{\left(\sqrt{\alpha_{hy}} + \sqrt{\alpha_{th}}\right)^2}{v_{seis}},$$

$$\delta_c = \frac{\rho c h}{f\Lambda}.$$

We also have the shear stress values at creep and seismic velocities (Equations 4.11 and 4.12):

$$\tau_{creep} = \sigma_{eff}\left[f^* + (a-b)\ln\left(\frac{v_{pl}}{V^*}\right)\right],$$

$$\tau_{seis} = \sigma_{eff}\left[f^* + (a-b)\ln\left(\frac{v_{seis}}{V^*}\right)\right].$$

We use the TP solutions from Equations 4.7 and 4.9 to define the slip required for a positive stress drop from TP for each end-member solution (Equations 4.13 and 4.14):

$$\delta_{drop}^{(c)} = \delta_c \ln\left(\frac{\tau_{seis}}{\tau_{creep}}\right)$$

$$\exp\left(\frac{\delta_{drop}^*}{L^*}\right)\mathrm{erfc}\left(\sqrt{\frac{\delta_{drop}^*}{L^*}}\right) = \frac{\tau_{creep}}{\tau_{seis}}.$$

Finally, we can use the ratio of the hydrothermal diffusion slip and the relevant δ_{drop} to determine the applicability range of each solution (Equations 4.17 and 4.19):

$$\frac{\delta_d}{\delta_{drop}^{(c)}} \approx 1.90\left(\frac{\delta_c}{L^*}\right),$$

$$\frac{\delta_d}{\delta_{drop}^*} \approx 3.28\left(\frac{\delta_c^2}{L^{*2}}\right).$$

We choose $\delta_{drop}^{(c)} < 0.1\delta_d$ for adiabatic, undrained solutions to be applicable, and $\delta_{drop}^* > 10\delta_d$ for slip-on-a-plane solutions to be applicable.

Our results suggest an approximate approach for considering the potential effect of different model parameters, including TP parameters, and different incoming seismic ruptures, without dynamic modeling, by comparing potential δ_{event} and analytically estimated δ_{drop}. Specifically:

- If $\delta_{event} > 10\delta_{drop}$, then full rupture.

- If $\delta_{drop} < \delta_{event} < 10\delta_{drop}$, then partial to full rupture.

- If $\delta_{event} < \delta_{drop}$, then no rupture.

where $\delta_{drop} = \delta_{drop}^*$ for the slip-on-a-plane regime and $\delta_{drop} = \delta_{drop}^{(c)}$ for the adiabatic, undrained regime.

Mw 7-Style Event
Slip-on-a-plane Model

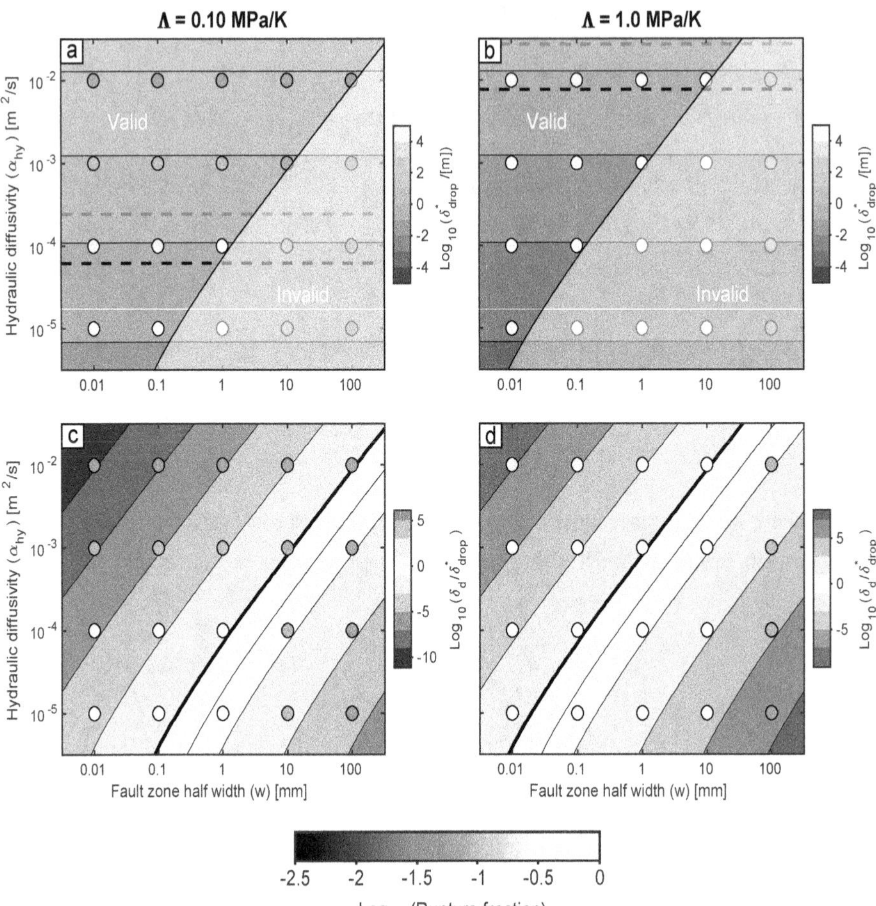

Figure 4.6: Variation in the slip δ^*_{drop} (top row) required for a positive stress drop, assuming the slip-on-a-plane solution, as we change TP parameters w, α_{hy} and Λ, and validity of the approximation (bottom row). The simulated rupture fraction values are also shown, for a M_w 7-style event. **(a)** Colorbar shows variation of δ^*_{drop} with w and α_{hy}, for $\Lambda = 0.1$ MPa/K. Each color change delineates an order of magnitude change in δ^*_{drop}, which only varies with α_{hy} given the assumption of an infinitesimally thin fault in the corresponding analytical solution. The approximation is expected to work for faults that are thin enough compared to diffusion time scales; this regime is highlighted with bright colors (see panel (c)), with the rest of the panel muted. The dashed black and red lines show where $\delta^*_{drop} = \delta_{event}$ for the M_w 6-style and M_w 7-style events, respectively. Note that, within the region of the validity of the analytical approximation (bright colors), the red dashed line predicts the transition from rupture propagation over the creeping section to rupture

arrest. **(b)** Same as (a), except with Λ increased by an order of magnitude to 1 MPa/K. This increased efficiency of TP results in δ^*_{drop} decreasing by two orders of magnitude for each value of α_{hy}. **(c)** Validity for the slip-on-a-plane approximation with $\Lambda = 0.1$ MPa/K. The colorbar shows variation of δ_d/δ^*_{drop}. The thick black contour delineates $\delta^*_{drop} = 10\delta_d$. The blue area to the left and top of this line satisfies $\delta^*_{drop} > 10\delta_d$, the range for which we take the slip-on-a-plane fault model to be a good approximation, as marked in (a). **(d)** Same as (c), except with $\Lambda = 1$ MPa/K. This increased efficiency of TP results in a reduced δ^*_{drop}, as shown in (b). This decrease causes the validity bound for the slip-on-a-plane approximation to shift to the left, reducing the number of our fault models that are well approximated by the slip-on-a-plane fault regime.

4.5 Discussion

4.5.1 Temperature Variation

Coffey et al. (2022) used measurements of biomarker thermal maturity from SAFOD samples to infer that peak temperatures on the fault had reached the range 570-1100 °C. They suggested that a large number of ruptures had broken the fault at this point in the creeping section. Based on assumptions about the evolution of friction during sliding, they calculated a slip range of 0.5-2.9 m associated with these peak temperatures. Our results provide a possible mechanism for these ruptures, consistent both with the arrest of M_w 6 ruptures, and the propagation of larger events with temperatures consistent with the results of Coffey et al. (2022).

For example, with $\Lambda = 0.34$ MPa/K, $w = 10$ mm and $\alpha_{hy} = 10^{-5}$ m^2/s, M_w 6-style events rapidly arrest in the creeping section, but M_w 7-style events are able to rupture all the way through. Figure 4.2 illustrates the evolution of the fault parameters with slip for a point on the creeping section at the approximate location of the SAFOD drill site in our model. As shown in Figure 4.2(f), TP allows for 4 meters of slip with a peak temperature change of 370 °C. Assuming an ambient temperature of 200 °C, representative of around 7 km depth, these results give a peak temperature of 570 °C, consistent with the measurements of Coffey et al. (2022).

However, the SAFOD samples are taken from 2.7 km depth, where ambient temperatures are closer to 110 °C (Lockner et al., 2011). We would also expect the stress state and efficiency of TP to vary with depth (Brantut & Platt, 2017), meaning our results cannot be straightforwardly applied to inferred rupture parameters at SAFOD. Our results do indicate how incorporating TP into the evolution of shear strength could allow for slip significantly greater than the 2.9 m upper bound calculated by Coffey et al. (2022), with peak temperatures still in their measured range.

Mw 7-Style Event
Adiabatic, Undrained Model

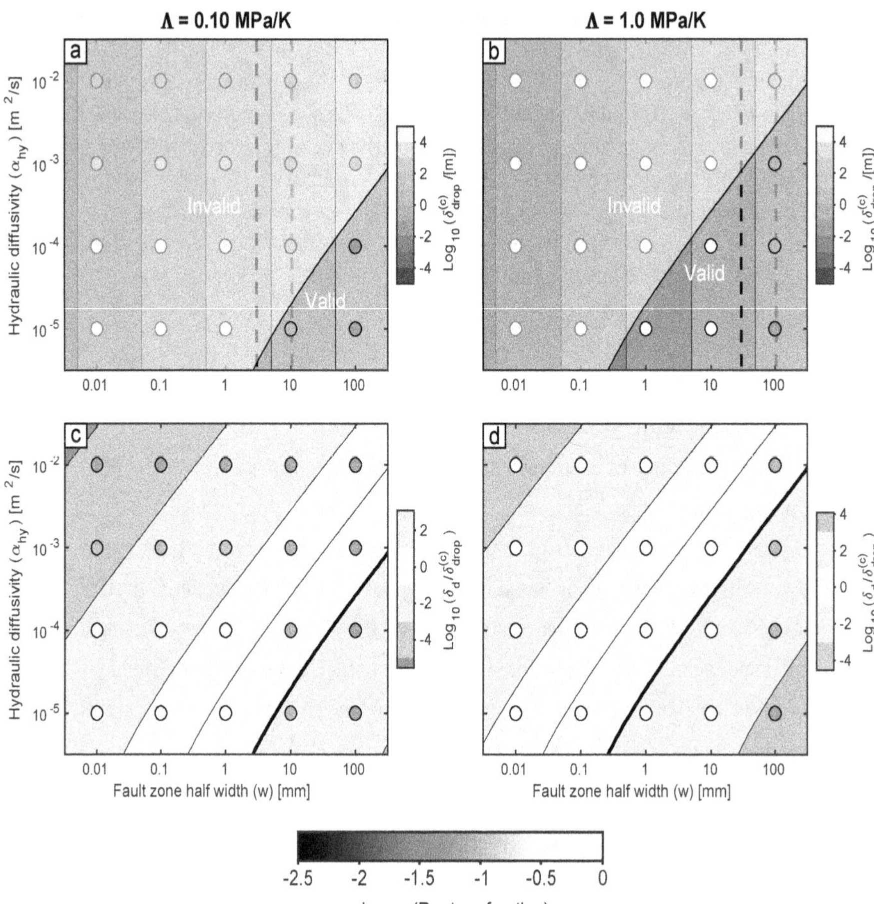

Figure 4.7: Same as Figure 4.6, except for the adiabatic, undrained fault solution (i.e. replacing δ^*_{drop} with $\delta^{(c)}_{drop}$). Note that the order of magnitude change in Λ between (a) and (b) causes an order of magnitude change in $\delta^{(c)}_{drop}$, compared to two orders of magnitude for δ^*_{drop} (shown in Figure 4.6). As the adiabatic, undrained fault solution assumes no transfer of fluid or heat out of the fault zone, $\delta^{(c)}_{drop}$ depends only on the fault zone width. The thick black contour in (c) and (d) now delineates $\delta^{(c)}_{drop} = 0.1\delta_d$; models to the right of this line satisfy $\delta^{(c)}_{drop} < 0.1\delta_d$, the range for which we take the adiabatic, undrained solution to be a good approximation to our models. As we go from (c) to (d), the increasing efficiency of TP results in a shorter $\delta^{(c)}_{drop}$, reducing the diffusion length scales and making more parameter combinations well approximated by the adiabatic, undrained regime. Similar to Figure 4.6, the red dashed line in (a) and (b) shows where $\delta^{(c)}_{drop} = \delta_{event}$ and marks a transition in the fraction of the creeping section ruptured.

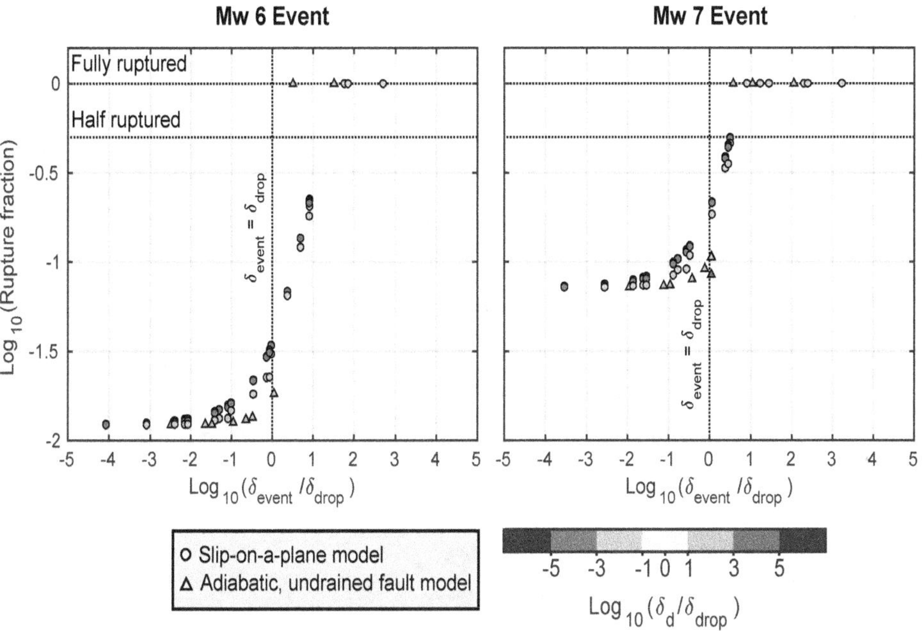

Figure 4.8: Logarithm of the fraction of the creeping section ruptured against the logarithm of the ratio between the total slip for the event in the absence of TP, δ_{event}, and the estimated slip required for a positive stress drop due to TP, δ_{drop}. For each combination of TP parameters, δ_{drop} is estimated for the slip-on-a-plane solution (δ^*_{drop}) and the adiabatic, undrained solution ($\delta^{(c)}_{drop}$). Only points for estimates that are expected to be good are plotted, defined by $\delta^{(c)}_{drop} < 0.1\delta_d$ and $\delta^*_{drop} > 10\delta_d$, as established based on Figures 4.6 and 4.7. Points with estimates of δ^*_{drop} outside of these validity bounds are plotted in Figure 4.9. The color of the symbols gives the log of the ratio between the hydrothermal diffusion distance, δ_d, and δ_{drop}, for the relevant end-member model. Values increasingly greater than 1 indicate that the fault model is increasingly closer to the adiabatic, undrained regime over the slip δ_{drop}, while values less than -1 indicate increasing closeness to the slip-on-a-plane fault regime. The line $\delta_{event} = \delta_{drop}$ captures the transition from ruptures arresting in the creeping region to increasingly large fraction of the creeping section being ruptured in our models.

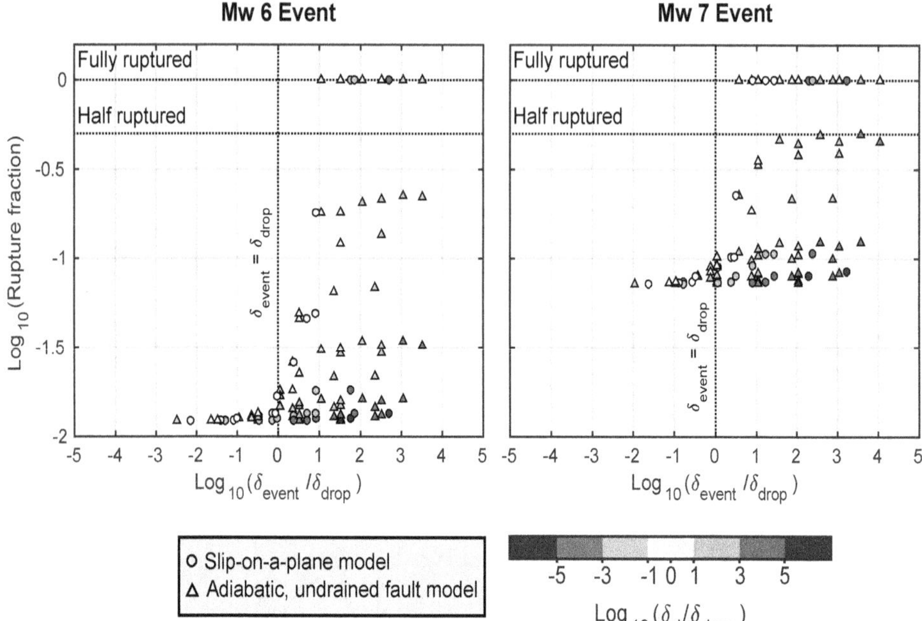

Figure 4.9: Same as Figure 4.8, except for estimates of δ_{drop} that are outside of the validity bounds we choose (i.e. $\delta_{drop}^{(c)} > 0.1\delta_d$ and $\delta_{drop}^* < 10\delta_d$).

For events that propagate into the creeping section in our simulations, the peak values of temperature can vary by two orders of magnitude. Lower TP efficiency, that is still sufficient to allow ruptures in the creeping section, promotes larger temperature rises. For some parameter combinations, the temperature change can peak at thousands of degrees, well past the melting threshold of around 1000 °C (Rice, 2006). Such high temperatures are inconsistent with the lack of melting observed in SAFOD cores (Coffey et al., 2022). The assumed fault constitutive law does not incorporate melting, so the onset of melting leads to a lack of self-consistency in our calculations (Noda & Lapusta, 2010). However, as long as the melting temperature is crossed towards the end of the slip, incorporating melting would likely not affect our overall results with regards to the fraction of the creeping section ruptured. Analyzing all our simulation results for peak and average temperatures reached is a subject of ongoing work.

Note that all of our simulations are consistent with the absence of heat anomaly around the SAF (Lachenbruch & Sass, 1980), since the average shear stresses acting on the creeping section in our models are within the corresponding constraint of 20 MPa. This stress is ensured by the choice of 0.15 as the reference friction coefficient and 120 MPa as the initial effective normal stress, which results in a steady-state value of shear stress at the plate rate in the creeping segment of about 15 MPa, with even lower values during thermal pressurization of pore fluids (e.g., Figure 4.2(a)).

4.5.2 Limitations of our Modeling

Our simplified modeling allows us to consider, in a tractable way, variations of several orders of magnitude in parameters that govern TP. However, the modeling does not account for a number of additional mechanisms that can affect rupture propagation and need to be investigated in future modeling.

As mentioned in the introduction, other dynamic weakening processes have been proposed, including flash heating, gel lubrication, nanoparticle lubrication, decarbonation, dehydration, and fault melting (Di Toro et al., 2011). Not all of these processes would necessarily occur in the clay rich fault gouge found in the creeping section in the SAF, but the conditions under which each mechanism is significant is an important component of future work.

Our models do not include fault dilatancy, which can accompany an increase in slip rate and lead to a drop in pore pressure, resulting in a reduced effective normal stress and increased fault strength (e.g., Segall and Rice (1995)). This effect would contribute to the peak shear resistance of the creeping section as the dynamic rupture enters it, requiring more efficient TP to produce positive stress drops for a given slip. Experimental results and theories of dilatancy are limited to the slow-slip regime and remain subject of active ongoing research; its role in shear, especially rapid, of the mature fault gouge found in the creeping section of the SAF remains uncertain (Brantut, 2020; Rice, 2006).

In order to capture different event styles in 2-D, we use two separate models for the M_w 6 and M_w 7-style ruptures. As a result of the different loading phases before rupture nucleation, the different event styles have different stress heterogeneities at the edge of the creeping section. A more realistic approach would be to capture both the M_w 6 and M_w 7-style events in a single 3-D model, allowing multiple M_w 6 events to rupture before a larger M_w 7 event occurred. 3-D models would also allow us to incorporate depth dependent properties. Such simulations would be much more computationally expensive, potentially requiring weeks of run time, making it challenging to explore a wide range of TP parameters given current computational constraints. The results of our 2-D parameter exploration can be the starting point for 3-D simulation, such as simulating the cases that arrest our simulated M_W 6-style event and allow our M_W 7-style event to propagate in 2-D.

Our simulated events have average slip rate of about 6 m/s, which is higher than the average of 1 m/s often cited for large events (Heaton, 1990). Higher slip rates increase the rate of shear heating and hence promote TP in models in which heat diffusion is important compared to the layer thickness, such as our fault models with very narrow shear layers that are well approximated by slip-on-a-plane solution (Figure 4.6). However, the effect would be more minor in fault models that are in the adiabatic, undrained regime (Figure 4.7), in which the weakening depends on total shear heat input and hence slip, and not as much on slip rate. Note that the fault model that provides a good match to the field results of Coffey et al. (2022) discussed in Section 4.5.1 is in the latter regime, and hence should not be much affected by its specific average slip rate. Considering the effect of incoming ruptures with different average slip rate (but the same slip) is a subject of ongoing work.

Our models assume a planar fault geometry, although the transition between the locked and creeping sections of the SAF is more complex, with the upper ~ 6 km of the fault showing a warp over a 50 km long section (Simpson et al., 2006). This geometry could act as a barrier to earthquake rupture, even in the presence of efficient TP. The fault is likely more planar at depth (Simpson et al., 2006), and even large stepovers in faults will not necessarily prevent rupture (H. Wang et al., 2020), so while the geometry may reduce the likelihood of rupture propagation for a given set of TP parameters, it would likely not eliminate it entirely.

Measurements at the SAFOD drill hole show that the fault is divided into two actively creeping strands, separated by less than 100 meters (Lockner et al., 2011). Coffey et al. (2022) found that the temperature rise from seismic slip was confined to a zone adjacent to one of the creeping strands of the fault, in a region previously identified as potentially having hosted seismic slip (Bradbury et al., 2011). Experimental tests by French et al. (2014) of SAFOD samples from one of the creeping strands showed dynamic weakening at seismic slip rates, which they attributed to TP. These observations highlight two possibilities, not considered by our model: 1) that a dynamic rupture could break two or more fault strands simultaneously, and 2) that the rupture could break a fault strand that is not actively creeping. If multiple, parallel, faults ruptured simultaneously that may result in lower slip rates and slips on each fault, reducing the amount of TP weakening. If the rupture follows an alternative path to the currently creeping sections, the rate-and-state parameters inferred for the properties of the creeping section, that we have assumed here, may not apply to the propagation of dynamic ruptures.

We keep the TP parameters constant in time; however, the evolution of TP parameters during an event can lead to significant changes in fault behavior. Rice et al. (2014) and Platt et al. (2014) argued that relatively wide shearing zones would be unstable, resulting in rapid shear localization to a narrow (5-40 μm) principle slip zone during seismic slip. That would imply evolving, and potentially decreasing, shear-zone width during an event, which could promote TP. Recent work by Stathas and Stefanou (2022) has suggested that the principle slip zone would not be stationary within the fault gouge at large slips, potentially resulting in oscillatory behavior in the frictional strength.

The coupling coefficient, Λ, and hydraulic diffusivity, α_{hy}, likely evolve during a rupture, both as a result of damage due to high stresses at the rupture tip, and changing pressure-temperature conditions (e.g., Aben et al. (2020), Badt et al. (2020), Brantut and Mitchell (2018), and Rice (2006)). Our parameters partially account for the effect of damage, as they include values taken from studies that approximated the effect of damage by modifications including increases to the fault gouge permeability and pore space compressibility from the lab-measured values, resulting in larger α_{hy} and lower Λ values, thus less efficient TP (e.g., Rice (2006)). Later work by Brantut and Mitchell (2018) suggested that these modifications gave a reasonable approximation for the impact of damage in faults which showed evidence of melting. To take account of parameter variation with pressure and temperature, Rice (2006) computed quantities averaged along representative pressure-temperature paths. Based on comparisons to solutions with pressure and temperature dependent properties in Rempel and Rice (2006), Rice (2006) argues that these path averages are a reasonable approximation.

The likely time scale and magnitude of the variation in parameters is important when considering the applicability of the models presented in this work. If the initial stress concentration at the rupture tip causes rapid damage-induced changes in TP properties, and further evolution, e.g., due to changes in pressure and temperature, is mild, then our use of fixed parameters during rupture could be justified. However, a larger event may create more significant damage due to higher stress concentrations, causing different events to be governed by different TP parameters. Fully incorporating these effects into modeling efforts would require a detailed understanding of how material properties evolve during rupture (e.g., Aben et al. (2020)).

4.5.3 Applicability of the Analytical Solutions

We apply analytical solutions for both slip on a mathematical plane and adiabatic, undrained conditions to gain physical insight into our simulations (Lachenbruch, 1980; Mase & Smith, 1987; Rice, 2006). Both solutions assume a constant coefficient of friction, f, and the thin fault solution assumes a constant seismic velocity, v_{seis}. To apply the analytical solutions, we set $f = 0.15$ and $v_{seis} = 6$ m/s. In the following, we discuss these choices and their limitations.

It is common to use a v_{seis} of 1 m/s in evaluating L^*, based on the results of Heaton (1990) (e.g., Noda and Lapusta (2013), Rempel and Rice (2006), and Rice (2006)). In our work, we have chosen 6 m/s, based on the average slip velocity on the edge of the velocity-weakening patch (discussed above). However, this average conceals substantial variation, with the slip velocity rapidly increasing to the limit of 15 m/s in under 5 cm of slip, remaining at the peak slip velocity for around 10 cm and 40 cm for the M_w 6 and M_w 7-style events, respectively, then decaying back down over the remaining slip.

The variation of slip velocity in the creeping section is highly dependent on the strength of the TP weakening. For strong TP, the slip velocity increase is even more rapid than within the velocity-weakening section; when TP is weaker the slip rate evolution is less abrupt; and there is no seismic slip over most of the creeping section when the TP falls below a certain threshold. The total slip of the incoming event, δ_{event}, the variation of the slip velocity during the event, and the ratio of δ_{event} to δ_{drop}, will all affect the most representative velocity to use when we look to understand when an event will propagate (see Figure 4.2 for an example). As the average slip rate over our events without TP is approximately 6 m/s, we use a value of $v_{seis} = 6$ m/s in the calculation of L^*; however, we acknowledge that our choice, and the assumption of constant velocity, are highly approximate.

The evolution of the rate-and-state friction coefficient, $f = \tau/\sigma_{eff}$, is governed by both by the slip rate and the rate-and-state characteristic slip distance D_{RS}. The most significant change is during the initial evolution from creep to seismic slip, where the friction coefficient jumps to a peak value (the direct effect), then evolves to a steady state value. By using a constant coefficient of friction when calculating L^* and δ_c, we assume both a constant slip velocity, and that the rate-and-state evolution of the friction coefficient occurs rapidly compared to the TP weakening, therefore allowing us to calculate δ_{drop} assuming steady-state sliding.

The slip over which the rate-and-state friction coefficient evolves from steady-state creep to steady-state seismic slip can be estimated from the equation (Bizzarri & Cocco, 2003):

$$D = D_{RS} \ln\left(\frac{v_{seis}}{v_{creep}}\right). \tag{4.21}$$

The creeping section moves at the plate rate, $v_{creep} = v_{pl} = 23$ mm/yr in steady state, and we set $v_{seis} = 6$ m/s, giving a value of $D \approx 20 D_{RS}$, or around 8 cm for our D_{RS} value of 4 mm.

We show an example of the evolution of stress within the creeping section in Figure 4.2(a). This simulation lies within the adiabatic, undrained regime, and the slip δ_{drop} needed to achieve positive stress drop in the creeping region should be well approximated by $\delta_{drop}^{(c)}$, which is ~56 cm. Figure 4.2(a) shows an initial quasi-linear weakening over < 10 cm of slip (governed by the state variable shown in Figure 4.2(e)), consistent with the estimate D of Equation 4.21, followed by ~ 40 cm of exponential decay in shear stress until it falls below its initial value, τ_{creep}. Hence the δ_{drop} from the numerical simulation is indeed well approximated by the analytically determined $\delta_{drop}^{(c)}$. In this case, RS friction evolves sufficiently faster than TP weakening to make $\delta_{drop}^{(c)}$ a reasonable approximation.

For parameter combinations leading to stronger TP, the TP weakening length scale can be comparable to, or less than, the rate-and-state evolution distance D. For example, for $\Lambda = 1$ MPa/K, $\alpha_{hy} = 10^{-5}$ m^2/s, and assuming $v_{seis} = 6$ m/s, $L^* \approx 4$ mm. When the TP and rate-and-state length scales are comparable, we can no longer assume that all rate-and-state friction evolution occurs before TP becomes relevant. The rate-and-state direct effect would therefore cause the TP weakening to begin from a higher stress, with a higher friction coefficient, than we assume in applying the analytical solution. TP with such a small slip-weakening scale as to be comparable to the rate-and-state evolution scales—much smaller than the incoming seismic slip—also implies very efficient TP, and all such fault models result in rupture propagation through the entire creeping section. The analytically inferred δ_{drop}^* would also be quite small, and hence the analytical solution would still predict propagation through the creeping region. Hence, this potential discrepancy between the actual and assumed friction coefficient for TP evolution does not have a significant impact on the results presented here.

4.6 Conclusions

We have investigated whether dynamic ruptures can propagate through the creeping section of the San Andreas Fault due to co-seismic thermal pressurization (TP) of pore fluids using a highly simplified 1-D fault model embedded in a 2-D elasto-dynamic medium. Our results show that, within the highly simplified framework of our model, a wide range of TP parameters cause a M_w 6-style event to rapidly arrest in the creeping section, but a M_w 7-style event to propagate partially or totally through.

Analytical solutions for TP show that the point at which events begin to substantially rupture the creeping section in our simulations is well explained by the requirement that the seismic slip in the incoming dynamic event is greater than the analytical estimates of slip needed for a positive stress drop due to TP in the otherwise velocity-strengthening creeping region. The full rupture of the creeping section always occurs in our simulations when the incoming seismic slip is 10 or more times larger than the analytical estimate of the slip needed for a positive stress drop. Our results suggest an approach for considering the potential effect of different model parameters, including TP parameters, and different incoming seismic ruptures, without dynamic modeling, by comparing potential slip during an event (δ_{event}) to an analytically estimated slip required for a positive stress drop (δ_{drop}). When applying the analytical solutions, it is important to consider the width of the diffusive zones in relation to the width of the shearing layer, to determine whether the slip-on-a-plane regime—in which heat and fluid diffusion are essential and accounted for—or the adiabatic, undrained regime is a good approximation.

These results suggest a mechanism for the creeping section of the San Andreas Fault to rupture during a major earthquake, offering a possible explanation for the inferred ruptures in the creeping section presented by Coffey et al. (2022). Further-more, we identify models with physically plausible parameters that have temperature increases in the range suggested by Coffey et al. (2022) and find that such ruptures can accumulate even larger seismic slip in the creeping section than estimated by Coffey et al. (2022). The parameters of such models include conservative choices for the efficiency of TP, such as low rate-and-state friction coefficients with the reference friction value of $f_* = 0.15$ (and the resulting "creeping" shear stress of

15 MPa; higher values would promote TP), time-independent TP parameters more appropriate for damaged rocks, such as hydraulic diffusivity of 10^{-4} to 10^{-5} m^2/s (using initial values for undamaged rocks may promote TP), and time-independent shear-layer width of 10 mm (whereas shear localization to narrower zones with slip may further promote TP). At the same time, our modeling does not include several ingredients that can reduce the efficiency of TP, including inelastic shear layer dilatancy and complex fault structure with multiple fault strands in the creeping region, which need to be investigated in future work.

Our work highlights the importance of further constraining fault physics through lab experiments coupled with computational and theoretical work, especially the evolution of hydraulic diffusivity, dilatancy, and shear-layer structure/width with ongoing seismic slip. Improved modeling of this problem would include expanding these simulations to 3-D in order to incorporate depth-dependent properties; incorporating dilatancy and evolution of TP parameters during the dynamic rupture; studying more realistic fault geometry; and including the possibility and effects of melting and other dynamic weakening mechanisms.

Table 4.1: Summary of simulation parameters. Parameters that we vary in this study are indicated in **bold** at the bottom, along with their ranges. DW: dynamic weakening. VW: velocity-weakening. VS: velocity-strengthening.

Parameter	Symbol	Value
Fault length	λ	200 km
Frictional fault length	λ_{fric}	180 km
Rate-and-state VW section length for M_w 6-style events	λ_{vw}	25 km
Crustal plane width for M_w 6-style events	H_{seis}	2 km
Rate-and-state VW section length for M_w 7-style events	λ_{vw}	80 km
Crustal plane width for M_w 7-style events	H_{seis}	8 km
Cell size	Δx	5 m
Plate loading rate	v_{pl}	23 mm/yr
Slip velocity limit	v_{lim}	15 m/s
P wave speed	c_p	5.2 km/s
S wave speed	c_s	3.0 km/s
Shear modulus	G	30 GPa
Poisson ratio	ν	0.25
Initial effective normal stress	$\sigma - p_0$	120 MPa
Rate-and-state reference slip velocity	V^*	10^{-6} m/s
Rate-and-state critical slip distance	D_{RS}	4 mm
	a	0.005
Rate-and-state properties in VW region	b	0.007
	f^*	0.3
	a	0.01
Rate-and-state properties in VS regions	b	0.006
	f^*	0.15
Specific heat	ρc	2.7 MPa/K
Thermal diffusivity in DW region	α_{th}	10^{-6} m²/s
Hydraulic diffusivity in DW region	α_{hyd}	$10^{-5} - 10^{-2}$ m²/s
Undrained dp/dT in DW region	Λ	0.01-1.0 MPa/K
Half-width of shear zone in DW region	w	0.01-100 mm

CONCLUSIONS AND OUTLOOK

This thesis has illustrated how we can draw on a diverse range of techniques to study the earthquake cycle over multiple temporal and spatial scales. We combined large InSAR data sets with modern processing techniques to study both the deformation of the Earth and the damage that earthquakes do over wide areas. Additionally, we used high-performance computational simulations of earthquakes, and analytical models, to explore how dynamic weakening via thermal pressurization can allow creeping sections of faults to rapidly rupture in earthquakes. Below, we review some suggestions for further work in each project, before providing some closing thoughts.

Our work in Chapter 1 showed how InSAR measurements can be corrected for the signal of plate motion. Until now, it has been common practice to either fit and remove the long-wavelength component of InSAR data, or use GNSS measurements to constrain the long-wavelength (e.g., Jolivet et al. (2015) and Weiss et al. (2020)). With the plate motion correction, combined with previously developed correction methods, it will be useful to explore how well InSAR can constrain very long-wavelength deformation without the aid of GNSS in a variety of different settings. The troposphere will likely be the dominant source of noise for time series spanning a few years (Parizzi et al., 2021), but with data spanning a decade or more the reduction in noise may be sufficient to recover long-wavelength secular signals below the level of 1 mm/yr, allowing greatly improved resolution in calculations of fault coupling.

The sensitivity to InSAR of plate motion also suggests that InSAR may be able to supplement GNSS data when constraining plate motion models, particularly in regions where GNSS is sparse. Given the small size of the plate motion signal, this would likely require long time series of InSAR data in order to get measurements of sufficient quality.

Using plate motion models to adjust InSAR data is roughly equivalent to expressing the InSAR measurements in a reference frame that is moving with the relevant plate. This correction may be less useful in zones of distributed deformation, for example, at plate motion boundaries, and how best to adjust InSAR measurements in this context, particularly without dense GNSS, is another important question that requires further study.

The results we presented for the Makran subduction zone in Chapter 2 show that, with plate motion corrections, as well as other adjustments, particularly for the ionosphere and troposphere, we are able to resolve tectonic deformation over a wide area with InSAR alone. While we were able to make broad statements about the degree of coupling on the megathrust, before such data can be fully interpreted we need more rigorous estimates of the noise levels (predominantly from residual troposphere) for our velocity measurements. Methods for estimating the noise in InSAR time series have already been developed (e.g., Agram and Simons, 2015; Lohman and Simons, 2005; Parizzi et al., 2021) and could be straightforwardly applied to our data, although we may need to take account of spatial variations in the noise. We also need to quantify the uncertainties introduced when we merge adjacent tracks in order to understand how well our merged velocity field is able to measure deformation spanning several tracks. It would also be sensible to experiment with more sophisticated approaches to merging tracks, for example incorporating data uncertainties and masking areas of known deformation when merging.

Our model of the subduction zone could also be improved, for example by using a layered elastic structure and updated fault geometry. There is some suggestion in the comparison between ascending and descending InSAR tracks that the convergence direction varies along the fault, with some amount of westward motion at the western end of the subduction zone, although this cannot be claimed with any certainty given our noise levels. Incorporating a variable convergence direction into our model might therefore be necessary. With the combination of an improved model and better estimates of the noise, it should be possible to invert the surface velocities for coupling on the megathrust. Using a Bayesian approach would allow a probabilistic coupling map to be derived (e.g., Lin et al. (2015)), revealing the impact of data and model uncertainties on the final coupling map, and the resulting uncertainties in the estimated size of potential future earthquakes.

The presence of significant post-seismic deformation at the eastern end of the subduction zone will likely make it challenging to invert for coupling in that region. Recent work has suggested that post-seismic deformation from the Balochistan earthquake is driven by creep on the megathrust (Lv & Shao, 2022), suggesting that the fault is fully decoupled north of 220 km from the deformation front of the accretionary prism. The eastern end is the only part of the megathrust to have hosted large earthquakes in historic time, making understanding coupling there an important issue. It may be possible to simultaneously invert for post-seismic deformation from the Khash and Balochistan earthquakes, as well as the coupling signal on the megathrust, possibly making use of the different temporal characteristics of post-seismic deformation and interseismic coupling, and the multiple different look directions provided by overlapping InSAR tracks. At the very least, a probabilistic inversion may be able to show us that the coupling cannot be resolved given the currently available data and ongoing post-seismic deformation.

Beyond our specific work, the clear hazard presented by the Makran subduction zone necessitates greater study from a variety of different angles. More geodetic work, ideally including the deployment of a dense network of GNSS stations on shore, and potentially ocean bottom geodesy, would allow for greater resolution of the megathrust coupling in space and time. Further work on measuring paleotsunamis is also necessary to piece together the seismic history of the western end of the subduction zone.

The damage mapping work of Chapter 3 showed how we could exploit part of the InSAR signal generally regarded as noise to rapidly map damage over wide areas. In our work, we quantify the quality of our damage classification using building damage data from the 2016 Amatrice earthquake. For this data set, every building in the town was inspected, and its level of damage recorded, allowing us to compute the precision and recall of our damage classifier. However, the data is limited to a small geographic region, and we cannot be sure if our method will maintain similar performance in other areas of the world. To ensure the reliability of this method, and test potential improvements, future work should focus on the development of high quality benchmarks—a global data set of natural disasters that are well covered by SAR data, and also have comprehensive damage assessments against which the classifier can be tested. Such benchmarks would allow our method to be tested across a wide range of conditions, providing more assurance that the method will perform well on future disasters. Organizations such as the Copernicus Emergency Management Service (https://emergency.copernicus.eu/), the Geotechnical Extreme Events Reconnaissance Association (https://geerassociation.org/), and the Humanitarian OpenStreetMap Team (https://www.hotosm.org/) may be useful places to look for damage mapping products and expertise.

There are several potential methodological developments that could also be explored, both in the input data, and damage classification algorithm, all of which could be tested against the benchmarks described above. The goal of the damage mapping algorithm is to get the best estimate of the probability distribution of the coherence under normal conditions, so that anomalies can be detected. To this end, the InSAR data could be augmented with spatial and temporal baselines, as well as potentially precipitation records, as these variables will all affect coherence, and could allow the deep learning algorithm to improve its forecast. Adding extra connections to the interferometric network, so that we have more than just sequential coherence images, may also be useful. Ultimately the best option may be to work directly with the amplitude and phase of the SLCs, rather than computing coherence.

On the algorithm side, it will be important to take advantage of the rapid progress in machine learning. The current method only makes use of individual time series when forecasting, meaning that potentially useful spatial correlations between adjacent time series are ignored. Architectures such as convolutional LSTMs allow spatial and temporal information to be incorporated when making forecasts (Shi et al., 2015); however, more recent developments in transformer architectures offer advantages over LSTM-based approaches (Vaswani et al., 2017; Zhou et al., 2021).

Rapid calculation of damage maps will benefit from quick coregistration of SAR images and computation of coherence. Currently, this process can be slow, particularly for large volumes of data, both because of processing and download times. Future work could therefore also go towards making these stages faster by improving the code, and deploying the code on high performance computers that can process many SAR images in parallel.

Along with technical work, efforts should also be made to better understand the requirements of end users, and how these damage maps can be integrated into existing emergency response pipelines. The ability to deliver timely products, in an understandable format, to emergency managers with whom there is a pre-existing relationship, is vital if these damage maps are to have practical applications. Important steps could include conducting interviews with disaster response experts, testing different data visualization approaches, and putting products on an easily accessible platform. It would be sensible to build on the knowledge of disaster response organizations that bridge the gap between scientists and emergency managers, such as the USGS Emergency Response (https://www.usgs.gov/emergency-operations-portal) and NASA's Disasters program (https://appliedsciences.nasa.gov/what-we-do/disasters). With these connections made, much of the mapping process could be automated, and products directly supplied to first responders with minimal outside intervention. The increasing availability of SAR data will hopefully make this possible within hours in the coming years.

Our dynamic rupture simulations presented in Chapter 4 highlighted the potential role of thermal pressurization in allowing the creeping section of the San Andreas Fault (SAF) to rupture co-seismically. Such results have important implications for the hazard posed by the SAF, and so require further investigation. The immediate development of this project could consist of extending the models to 3-D, and incorporating a wider variety of physical processes in to the model. A 3-D model would allow M_w 6 and M_w 7-style events to be simulated together, although this would present substantial computational challenges. It may be necessary to reduce the computational burden, for example by substantially truncating the size of the creeping section and M_w 7 patch, in order to explore parameter combinations in a manageable amount of time. The use of 2-D models and analytical solutions will be important in narrowing the parameter space.

Direct experimental observations of thermal pressurization in laboratory settings remain limited, the parameters controlling its efficiency are highly uncertain, and the the situations under which other weakening mechanisms could dominate are unclear (e.g., Aben et al., 2020; Badt et al., 2020; Brantut and Mitchell, 2018). Modeling efforts rely on physical observations to determine the relevant processes, but can also inform future experiments by indicating which parameter uncertainties have the greatest influence on the model behavior. Our modeling work has highlighted several particularly important parameters, and future experimental work should be able to place better constraints on these.

The coming decade will see a continual increase in the availability of data and computing power, promising exciting new results, but also many potential pitfalls. In 1810, German polymath Johann Wolfgang von Goethe stated:

> "The modern age has a false sense of superiority, because of the great mass of data at its disposal. But the valid criterion of distinction is rather the extent to which [humanity] knows how to form and master the material at [its] command."[1]

Goethe's words are a reminder that it is not just humanity's ability to collect and process large volumes of data that pushes forward our understanding of the world,

---

[1] This quote sits on my advisor's wall, and is generally attributed to Goethe's "Theory of Colors," published in 1810 in German, with an English translation appearing in 1840. I have been unable to find a direct version of this quote in the 1840 translation, but the quote is attributed to Goethe by the 1949 book "Goethe: Wisdom and Experience." I therefore include the attribution with some caution. As Abraham Lincoln famously said: "Remember that not everything you read on the internet is true."

but also our ability to intelligently "form and master" the material at our command, combining insights from the smallest to the largest scales to tell a coherent story about our Earth.

The scientific advances to come promise profound benefits to humanity, but it is ultimately a question of politics and policy that determines how they will be used. In this thesis we have examined natural processes that can lead to enormous destruction, but there are no natural disasters. Who lives and who dies, which buildings collapse and which remain standing—these are questions that depend on the decisions made by those with power. These decisions must be informed by the best science, *and* made for the benefit of everyone. It is to this endeavor that I now turn my attention.